JANET FRAME

To the Is-Land

Autobiography 1

PALADIN
GRAFTON BOOKS
A Division of the Collins Publishing Group

LONDON GLASGOW
TORONTO SYDNEY AUCKLAND

Paladin
Grafton Books
A Division of the Collins Publishing Group
8 Grafton Street, London W1X 3LA

Published in Paladin Books 1987
9 8 7 6 5 4 3 2

First published in Great Britain by
The Women's Press 1983

ISBN 0-586-08585-8

Printed and bound in Great Britain by
Collins, Glasgow

Set in Ehrhardt

This first volume
is dedicated to my parents
and brother and sisters

Acknowledgements

Grateful acknowledgement for the continuing support of the New Zealand Literary Fund, my friends and publisher.

Grateful acknowledgement is also made to the following for permission to reprint selected verse passages:

Extract from 'I met Eve' by Walter de la Mare, reprinted by permission of The Literary Trustees of Walter de la Mare and The Society of Authors as their representative;

Extract from 'Old Grey Squirrel' by Alfred Noyes, reprinted with the permission of William Blackwood & Sons Limited and the author's estate.

Janet Frame was born in Dunedin, New Zealand, in 1924. Her works include ten novels, among them *Owls Do Cry*, *A State of Siege*, *Scented Gardens for the Blind*, *Yellow Flowers in the Antipodean Room*, *Faces in the Water* and *Living in the Maniototo*, which won the Fiction Prize, New Zealand Book Awards, 1980. She has also had published four collections of stories and sketches, a volume of poetry and a children's book, *Mona Minim and the Smell of the Sun*. Janet Frame has won a number of distinctions in her native country and was awarded a CBE in the 1983 Queen's Birthday Honours List. She is New Zealand's most distinguished living novelist.

To the Is-Land is the first volume of her autobiography, and won the New Zealand literary prize the James Wattie Book of the Year award in 1983.

Index of Chapters

1

In the Second Place

From the first place of liquid darkness, within the second place of air and light, I set down the following record with its mixture of fact and truths and memories of truths and its direction always toward the Third Place, where the starting point is myth.

2

Toward the Is-Land

The Ancestors – who were they, the myth and the reality? As a child, I used to boast that the Frames 'came over with William of Orange.' I have since learned that this may have been so, for Frame is a version of Fleming, Flamand, from the Flemish weavers who settled in the lowlands of Scotland in the fourteenth century. I strengthen the reality or the myth of those ancestors each time I recall that Grandma Frame began working in a Paisley cotton mill when she was eight years old; that her daughters Polly, Isy, Maggie spent their working lives as dressmakers and in their leisure produced exquisite embroidery, knitting, tatting, crochet; and that her son George Samuel, my father, had a range of skills that included embroidery (or 'fancy-work,' as it was known), rug making, leatherwork, painting in oils on canvas and on velvet. The Frames had a passion for making things. Like his father, our Grandad Frame, a blacksmith who made our fire pokers, the boot-last, and even the wooden spurtle smoothed with stirring the morning porridge, my father survives as a presence in such objects as a leather workbag, a pair of ribbed butter pats, a handful of salmon spoons.

As children, we heard little of our father's ancestors, the Frames and the Patersons, only that most had immigrated to the United States of America and to Canada, where 'Cousin Peg' became a schoolteacher. And none remains now of that Frame family of eight sons – John, Alex, Thomas, Robert, William Francis, Walter Henry, George Samuel, Charles Allan – and four daughters – Margaret, Mary, Isabella Woods. The fourth, my namesake, died at thirteen months.

Mother's family, the Godfreys, had long been established in Wairau and Blenheim and Picton, where Mother, Lottie Clarice, was born and brought up in a family of three brothers – Charles, Lance, William – and five sisters – May, Elsie, Joy, Grace,

Jessie (who died in her twenty-first year). Mother's father, Alfred Godfrey, also a blacksmith, was the son of John Godfrey, a political character known as 'The Duke,' who owned the Sheepskin Tavern in Wairau Valley and was later editor of the Marlborough Press. We heard from Mother of John Godfrey's brother Henry and of their father, an Oxford doctor, whose 'Godfrey's Elixir' was known in Great Britain in the early nineteenth century; of Mother's mother, Jessie Joyce, from a Jersey Islands family of French origin, and her mother, Charlotte, formerly Charlotte Nash, author of the poems in a small book with an engraved cover and sweet-pea-colored pages, written at eighteen, before her emigration from Harbledown, Kent, to New Zealand – Charlotte, whose second marriage was to James or 'Worser' Heberley, of Worser Bay, Wellington, given to him by the tribe of his first wife (Te Atiawa).

Mother and Father, then. Mother leaving school early to become a dental nurse at Mr Stocker's rooms in Picton, later to be a housemaid in various homes in Picton and Wellington – the Beauchamps, the Loughnins – and, during the Great War, in the early years of her marriage, in the home of Wili Fels in Dunedin; Mother, a rememberer and talker, partly exiled from her family through her marriage out of the Christadelphian faith and her distance from Marlborough, remembering her past as an exile remembers her homeland; Mother in a constent state of family immersion even to the material evidence of the wet patch in front of her dress where she leaned over the sink, washing dishes, or over the copper and washtub, or, kneeling, wiped the floor with oddly shaped floorcloths – old pyjama legs, arms and tails of worn shirts – or, to keep at bay the headache and tiredness of the hot summer, the vinegar-soaked rag she wrapped around her forehead: an immersion so deep that it achieved the opposite effect of making her seem to be seldom at home, in the present tense, or like an unreal person with her real self washed away. Perhaps we were jealous of the space that another world and another time occupied in our mother's life; and although, perhaps fearing immersion in this foreign world, we struggled to escape, we were haunted by her tales of the Guards, the Heberleys, Diffenbach, shipwrecks in the Sounds, life in Waikawa Road and down the Maori pah, family life at the Godfreys', remembered as paradisal. We came to know by heart incidents reported with exact conversations at school, at home, in the dentist's rooms, and in the homes where Mother worked – from her excitement on her first day at school at seeing a weta crawling on brother Willy's knee ('Oooh, look on Willy's knee!') to the words of Mr Loughnin the magistrate as he (in nightshirt and nightcap) lured his wife to his bed with 'Letty, I want you . . .'

When Mother talked of the present, however, bringing her sense of wondrous contemplation to the ordinary world we knew, we listened, feeling the mystery and the magic. She had only to say of any commonplace object, 'Look, kiddies, a stone' to fill that stone with a wonder as if it were a holy object. She was able to imbue every insect, blade of grass, flower, the dangers and grandeurs of weather and the seasons, with a memorable importance along with a kind of uncertainty and humility that led us to ponder and try to discover the heart of everything. Mother, fond of poetry and reading, writing, and reciting it, communicated to us that same feeling about the world of the written and spoken word.

Father, known to us as 'Dad,' was inclined to dourness with a strong sense of formal behavior that did not allow him the luxury of reminiscence. One of the few exceptions was his tales of 'the time we had the monkey,' told with remembered delight and some longing. When his family left Oamaru, where he was born, to live in Port Chalmers (where his mother, Grandma Frame, became known as midwife), Grandad Frame brought home from the pub a monkey left by one of the sailors. 'Tell us,' we used to say to Dad, 'about the time you had a pet monkey.'

Dad, too, left school early, although he was a good student, as the class photos of 'Good Workers at Albany Street School' testify. His first job was making sound effects (horses galloping and wild storm sounds) at the local theater, and his first adventure was his attempt to fly from the roof of the family house in Dunedin. Later he began work on the railway as a cleaner, progressing to fireman, second-class engine driver, which was his occupation when I first met him, later to first-class engine driver, following the example of his brothers who spent their lives with engines and movement – Alex, who became a taxi driver; Wattie, a sea captain, later a harbor master in Newport, Melbourne; Charlie, who was for a time a motor mechanic and chauffeur to Sir Truby King. Brother Bob became a baker in Mosgiel.

Mum and Dad (Mother was known as 'Mum' until I considered

myself grown up enough to acknowledge her as a separate personality) were married at the Registry Office in Picton three weeks
before Dad sailed to the Great War. When Dad returned from the
war, he and Mother set up house in Richardson Street, St Kilda,
Dunedin, helped by a rehabilitation loan of twenty-five pounds
with which they bought one wooden kerb, one hearth rug, two
morris dining chairs, one duchesse, one oval dining table, one iron
bedstead and flock mattress, one kitchen mat, these items being
listed on the document of loan with a chilling reminder that while
the loan remained unpaid, the king's representative (the agreement
was between 'His Majesty the King and George Samuel Frame')
had the right to enter the Frame household to inspect and report
on the condition of the 'said furniture and fittings.' The loan was
repaid after a few years, and the document of discharge kept by my
parents in their most hallowed keeping place – the top right-hand
drawer of the king's duchesse – where were also kept my sister
Isabel's caul, Mother's wedding ring, which did not fit, her upper
false teeth, which also did not fit, Myrtle's twenty-two-karat gold
locket engraved with her name, and Dad's foreign coins, mostly
Egyptian, brought home from the war.

There were the ancestors, then, given as mythical possessions –
your great-grandmother, your great-grandfather, did this, was this,
lived and died there and there – and the living parents, accumulating memories we had not shared. Then on 15 December 1920, a
daughter, Myrtle, was born, and on 20 April 1922, a son, Robert,
or Bruddie; in 1923 another son, stillborn, unnamed, was buried;
and on 28 August 1924, I was born, named Janet Paterson Frame,
with ready-made parents and a sister and brother who had already
begun their store of experience, inaccessible to me except through
their language and the record, always slightly different, of our
mother and father, and as each member of the family was born,
each, in a sense with memories on loan, began to supply the
individual furnishings of each Was-Land, each Is-Land, and the
hopes and dreams of the Future.

3

In Velvet Gown

I was delivered by Dr Emily Seideberg McKinnon at St Helens Hospital, Dunedin, where I was known as 'the baby who was always hungry.' I had a twin, which did not develop beyond a few weeks. Twins were hereditary in Mother's family, and she would often quote the poem written by (I think) her grandmother, whose two sets of twins died in infancy: 'Four little locks of gold.' Mother's memory of my birth always had two repeated references – her boast that I was delivered by the first woman medical graduate in New Zealand and her pride in the abundance of milk that enabled her to feed myself and other babies.

'My milk was drawn off,' she'd say, making a liberal giving motion toward and away from her 'titties,' in one of her many gestures that we, the ancestors ever alert beside us, assigned to the 'French' side of the family. With similar drama Mother spoke of *Dr Emily Seideberg McKinnon*, which must have impressed me even during my first few days of being, for her lifelong repetition of names important to her – Henry Wadsworth Longfellow, Harriet Beecher Stowe, John Greenleaf Whittier, William Pember Reeves (*The Passing of the Forest*), Michael Joseph Savage – never failed to awaken a sense of magic.

I was born into a town that had lately known two historic events and was preparing for others. In 1923 the low-lying parts of Dunedin and St Kilda, where we lived, were severely flooded by the Leith, while a few years earlier the Prince of Wales had visited Dunedin. My earliest recollections, therefore, are of the talk of the prince and the flood and of the inaccessibility of the talk, so far above me, to and fro, to and fro between tall, tall people. When I was three weeks old, the family shifted to Outram, where we had a house with a big walnut tree at the back and a cow byre with a red and white branchy-horned Ayrshire cow named Betty; and when I was six weeks old, I was in the cow byre with Mother while she milked Betty. My earliest memories are fragmentary and apart from the talking of the adults are all set outside – in the cow byre, in the neighbor's orchard, under the walnut tree where, as I grew, I was put in a huge kerosene box to play and where I learned to walk, first holding on to the rim of the box. I was told that my first words were 'Pick walnut up, Mummy,' pronouncing *walnut* as 'warnut.' My pronunciation was usually incorrect and apparently amused everyone. A sty in my eye was cured by the 'pitties,' not, as I was told, by the *pixies*. I sang, 'God Save our Gracious *Tin*.' I drank 'Mook.' The new baby that came when I was twenty months old and was named Isabel became, for me, 'Iddabull.'

It was while Mother was busy with the new baby that Grandma Frame, who lived with us, became my companion and friend. It was she who told me about the 'pitties.' I remember her first as a tall woman in a long, black dress and later, when her diabetes forced the amputation of one of her legs, in her wheelchair. Her skin was dark, her black hair frizzy, and although she talked in Scottish, the songs she sang were of the American Deep South. She'd be going silently about the house when suddenly her voice would come out in a singing that filled me with the kind of feeling I learned much later to identify as sadness. 'Carry me back to ole Virginny . . .,' Grandma sang, pausing after the first line as if she were almost there but needed a natural delay to transport her whole being. I know I could see it in the way she looked around the room as if she were suddenly a stranger and might even remark, as strangers did, 'Oh, you've got one of these, Lottie. I didn't know you had one of these. They're nice to have, aren't they?' But Grandma was away in the song, 'That's where the cotton and the corn and taters grow . . .' She sang of 'Laboring hard for Ole Massa.' I assumed that Grandma Frame was African and had been a slave in America, that her real home was 'Virginny,' where she longed to return; for you see I knew about slaves.

The book that everyone was talking about in our house was *Uncle Tom's Cabin*, by Harriet Beecher Stowe, and I was being called Topsy because my hair was frizzy. 'Who are you?' they'd ask me, and I learned to reply 'I'm the girl that never was born pras I grew up among the corn. Golly. Aint I wicked!' Mother talked, too, of Eliza crossing the ice as if it had really happened, like the pioneers and the visit of the prince and the flood. She talked of wicked Simon Legree. There was much talk of ice, of sheet ice and pack ice and icebergs, for the *Titanic* disaster was often mentioned, still uppermost in people's minds.

Those Outram days until my third birthday give isolated memories and feelings: of the hours I spent watching Betty the cow with her skin-covered machinery working at both ends – all the smells and colors and diversity of solids (turnips and apples) and liquids taken in at one end and let out the other. I'd stand in front of the bail, feeding her the big, red apples, and from time to time she'd open her mouth and yawn, flooding her potato-and-turnip-and-apple-and-grass-smelling breath into my face and showing her big, worn-down teeth. I remember the Snows and their orchard, my small friend Bobby Little, who taught me to say *bugger*, which I called 'Budda.' I remember the terrible magazine, which was not to be approached – at the back of the drill hall (or wi'hall, as I called it) – and the shining silver kerosene tin, which was my only toy, which I pulled on a length of string after me wherever I went, while it clanged and rattled and sometimes dented in one side then popped or dinked, returning to its old shape, making the sound the rain made inside the water tank. I remember Topsy and Simon Legree and Eliza on the ice and the bogies (or 'bodies'), who came after dark when the candles were pinched out and the wick turned down on the kerosene lamp, and I remember, as my earliest memory, something that could not have happened: a tall woman wearing a clothes peg on her nose peered into the bedroom from a small window high in the wall and, looking down at me in my wooden cot, said sharply, 'You're a nosey-parker.'

My most vivid memory of that time is the long, white dusty road outside the gate, the swamp (which I called the 'womp'), which filled me with terror, for I had been warned never to go near it, and the strange unnaturally bright green grass growing around it and the weeds like the inside of the India rubber ball growing along its surface and the golden beastie in a velvet coat grazing near the fence – and of myself wearing my most treasured possession, a golden velvet dress, which I named my 'beastie' dress. I remember a gray day when I stood by the gate and listened to the wind in the telegraph wires. I had my first conscious feeling of an outside sadness, or it seemed to come from outside, from the sound of the wind moaning in the wires. I looked up and down the white dusty road and saw no one. The wind was blowing from place to place past us, and I was there, in between, listening. I felt a burden of sadness and loneliness as if something had happened or begun and I knew about it. I don't think I had yet thought of myself as a person looking out at the world; until then, I felt I *was* the world. In listening to the wind and its sad song, I knew I was listening to a sadness that had no relation to me, which belonged to the world.

I don't attempt to search for the commonplace origins of such a feeling. When you bring home a shell treasure from the beach, you shake free the sand and the mesh of seaweed and the other crumbled pieces of shell and perhaps even the tiny dead black-eyed inhabitant. I may have polished this shell of memory with the application of time but only because it is constantly with me, not because I have varnished it for display.

I was learning words, believing from the beginning that words meant what they said. I was slightly puzzled that there should be a railway magazine in the house when we children were forbidden to go near the magazine. And when I sang 'God Save Our Gracious Tin,' I believed that I was singing about my cherished kerosene tin. In the Outram days, when many relatives lived near, there was much coming and going and talking and laughing, with words traveling like the wind along the invisible wires, words full of meaning and importance describing the Great Dunedin and South Seas Exhibition and the visit of the Duke of York and naming places. The relatives who visited were mostly the Frames, an excitable family with a passion for detail and a love of home and hearth that helped to make the smallest expedition beyond the home an occasion to recall in minute detail all the meetings, conversations, news, rumors, and actual events, and when the events were as important as royal visits and great exhibitions and floods and the sinking of unsinkable ships, mixed with dramatic details of books being read and poems remembered as if they, too, had been present occasions, then I can explain the sense of excitement I felt but could not understand as it moved to and fro in the traveling network of words.

But we were railway people. And when I was three, we shifted house to Glenham in Southland.

4

The Railway People

My memory is once again of the colors and spaces and natural features of the outside world. On our first week in our Glenham house on the hill, I discovered a place, *my place*. Exploring by myself, I found a secret place among old, fallen trees by a tiny creek, with a moss-covered log to sit on while the new-leaved branches of the silver birch tree formed a roof shutting out the sky except for the patterned holes of sunlight. The ground was covered with masses of old, used leaves, squelchy, slippery, wet. I sat on the log and looked around myself. I was overcome by a delicious feeling of discovery, of gratitude, of possession. I knew that this place was entirely *mine*; mine the moss, the creek, the log, the secrecy. It was a new kind of possession quite different from my beastie dress or from the new baby Isabel, over whom Myrtle and Bruddie and I argued so often (for Mother had said that Isabel was *my* baby, just as Bruddie was Myrtle's baby) that it seemed to me that owning people was too hard to manage if you had to keep fighting over possession.

I remembered my overwhelming sense of anticipation and excitement at the world – the world being My Place by the fallen birch log, with the grass, the insects in the grass, the sky, the sheep and cows and rabbits, the wax-eyes and the hawks – everything Outside. I remember my special feeling for the sky, its faraway aboveness, up there where my mother and father lived, and the way I was filled with longing for it, a kind of nostalgia shared by my brother and sisters some years later when we discovered an old schoolbook with a poem that began:

> On his back in the meadow a little boy lay
> with his face turned up to the sky
> and he watched the clouds as one by one
> they lazily floated by . . .

We lay together in the long summer grass, looking up at the clouds, reciting the poem, and knowing that each was feeling the same homesickness and longing for the sky.

This passion for the outside world was strengthened by the many journeys we made in Dad's gray Lizzie Ford to rivers and seas in the South, for Dad was a keen fisherman, and while he fished, we played and picnicked and told stories, following the example of Mother, who also composed poems and stories while we waited for the billy to boil over the manuka fire. On one of those early expeditions to the south coast, I told my story of the bird and the hawk and the bogie (pronounced by me 'birdie,' 'hawt,' 'bodie'), and although the telling of the story is a reinforced memory as Mother often recalled it, mimicking even my gesture of sympathy as I put my head on one side and said, 'Oh! poor little birdie,' I do remember the occasion chiefly because I remember seeing in my mind the huge, dark shadow of the bogie as it came from behind the hill: 'Once upon a time there was a birdie. One day a hawt flew out of the sky and at the birdie. (Oh poor little birdie.) The next day a bid bodie came out from behind the hill and ate up the hawt from eating up the little birdie.'

I remember, too, the fierce attempt to *make* my audience, Myrtle and Bruddie, sit absolutely still and my asking Mother for help. 'Mum, Myrtle and Bruddie's wiggling. Tell them to stop wiggling while I tell my 'tory.'

The poems that Mother recited to us on those picnics were prompted by the surroundings – the lighthouse at Waipapa, the Aurora Australis in the sky. 'Look, the Southern lights, kiddies.'

> The lighthouse on the rocky shore
> the seagulls' lonely cry
> and day departing leaves behind
> God's picture in the sky.

There were other poems that Mother had not composed herself – tales of shipwreck, of tidal waves: 'High Tide on the Coast of Lincolnshire,' 'Come up, Whitefoot, come up, Lightfoot, Jetty to the milking shed ...' Well, we knew about cows, and we knew about floods. 'When Myrtle and Bruddie were little, before you were born, Nini.' We'd had to 'give up' Betty when we shifted from Outram, and we now bought our milk from Mr Bennett on the hill opposite. We learned to love those beaches and rivers and the long shadows of a Southland twilight and the golden roads lit on each side by the gorse hedges and the ever-present hawks circling in the sky.

Myrtle and Bruddie started school at Glenham, and sometimes I went with them to the one-teacher school on top of yet another hill, and I sat in a corner, watching and listening to the 'big people.' I learned a special word at Glenham – *gored* – following a time of drama when Mr Bennett was *gored* by his dark brown Jersey bull and rushed to Invercargill Hospital, and everyone said the dark brown Jersey bulls were the fiercest.

I spent much time, too, at 'my place,' enjoying its being there. Then one night Dad came home with his news: 'I've got a shift, Mum. To Edendale.' The arrangement was that we were to shift in the early summer, and in the meantime (it was now autumn) our railway house was to be pulled down and rebuilt at Edendale while we spent the winter in railway huts in the paddock overlooked by the school and the Bennetts' and our house: a paddock with a swamp in the corner and bulrushes and snowberries and penny oranges growing in the silken snowgrass.

Swamp red, beastie gold, sky gray, railway-red, railway-yellow, Macrocarpa green, tussock gold, snowgrass gold, penny-orange orange, milk-white snowberry white, all lit by the sky of snow light reflected from Antarctica or, as we knew it, from Mother's constant reference, 'the South Pole, kiddies.' These colors filled my seeing and our excitement at the prospect of living *Outside*.

There were three railway huts (possibly a fourth, with a copper, to be used as a washhouse): a kitchen-living hut, a bedroom hut with bunks for Myrtle, Bruddie, and me, a bedroom hut for Mum and Dad and the baby Isabel, each hut being about six feet by eight feet, except for the slightly larger kitchen-living hut, which had a stove with a tin chimney poking through the roof. Each hut was painted railway red and had its own door. The lavatory, or 'dumpy,' as we called it, was the usual enclosure about a deep hole, with a railway-red seat. Our lighting was by candle and kerosene, and only the kitchen hut had a stove. The anticipated delights, intensified by Mother's ability to pluck poetic references from those many rooted in her mind, began to die with the first touch of the Southland blizzard. Tales of gypsy camps, or Arabs folding their tents, of Babes in the Wood, could scarcely defeat the bitter cold. It seemed to be always snowing with the snow lying deep around the huts and in the central courtyard.

I think I knew unhappiness for the first time. I was miserable, locked away each night from Mum and Dad and unable to reach them except by going through the snow. I was at an age to be teased, and because I had let it be known that I was afraid of rats in the wall, I was teased with cries of rats in the wall, rats in the wall. We were all sick, with colds, and I began to suffer the pains in my legs that became part of my childhood. I was feverish and delirious, seeing insects crawling up and down the wall. The 'growing pains' and the fever were rheumatic fever. Everywhere was damp and cold, and the world was full of damp washing and nappies covered with green mess as if the baby, like a calf, had been eating grass. Mum was still breast-feeding Isabel. I had stopped feeding when I was two and had started biting, although Mother's titties were always there, like the cow's teats for an occasional squirt into our mouths. Yet, while Mother 'believed' in breast-feeding her children for as long as possible, she also took pride in our early use of cups and knives, forks and spoons. She would say proudly of me that I was 'drinking from a cup at six weeks.' When she finally wanted us to know that her titties were not for us but for the newest baby, she smeared a bitter substance over her breasts.

In spite of the misery of Inside, the times around the kitchen stove were cozy, and bathing in the round, tin bath in front of the stove – rub a dub dub three men in a tub – was always pleasant. And Mother, as was to become her habit, helped to lighten our (and no doubt her) misery by pointing out the beauty of the snow and telling us stories of the snow and the rain and Jack Frost, who was 'after our fingers and toes.' She'd look out into the country-black dark through the small, chill uncurtained window of the hut and murmur, 'I wonder is Jack Frost coming tonight ...' She knew and we knew that he came every night, but I was fascinated by the reference to him as a person with a name, and I think I believed in his existence more surely than I ever believed in that other night traveler, Santa Claus. Also, in the warm of the kitchen hut Mother would play her accordion and sing while Dad, sometimes striding up and down in the snow (he insisted that you had to stride up and down while you played the bagpipes), played his bagpipe tunes – 'The Cock o' the North' or 'The Flowers of the Forest' or others from his book of bagpipe music.

It was late summer when we shifted into our rebuilt house at Edendale, into the heart of our railway country – beside the railway line and the goods shed and the engine shed and the turntable and the points and the watertank painted railway hut red on its railway-hut-red stand beside the railway line and the spindly red-painted little house high up where the signalman lived and hung out his signals and the resting or retired railway carriages and trucks and trolleys. Among our games was 'trolley works,' where we pretended to be trolleys on the railway line. I spent much time playing around the railway territory among the railway weeds and flowers – dock and wild sweet peas – and in the goods shed, where the sacks of grain were piled high and I, suddenly powerful as a 'jackdaw,' climbed to the top of the sacks, or 'climbers' as we knew them, and swooped down upon Myrtle and Bruddie, flapping my wings and making a hawklike cry. 'Nini's the jackdaw,' they said at meals when Mum or Dad asked what we'd been doing. 'Nini's the jackdaw, and we've been climbing up the climbers.' I'd not seen jackdaws, but I'd heard stories of the way they swooped upon bright objects to carry them to their nest.

It seemed that we had scarcely settled in our new-old house when word came that we were to shift once again – to Wyndham.

5

Ferry Street, Wyndham

Wyndham, the Southland town of rivers, with our house the usual kind of railway house by the railway line but this time in a street with a name – Ferry Street – which I interpreted as *Fairy* Street. From a pixie-inhabited Outram to a fairy-filled Wyndham did not seem like a misuse of logic and experience. In Wyndham I discovered that the world held more people than I had dreamed of – I'd thought of the world as all sky, green paddocks, swamps, bulrushes, tussock, snowgrass, sheep, cattle; and the wind in the telegraph wires along deserted roads; and the railway coming from and going to; and one or two neighbors who gave us milk and apples in exchange for some of Dad's fish – rainbow and brown trout, whitebait, oysters – or our kinds of plums and apples; and people, especially in Outram, as relations, coming and going and talking of up Central and Middlemarch and Inch Clutha; and then, as in Glenham and Edendale, the world as a place where we lived alone with the weather; with our mother and father working all day and singing and playing the accordion and the bagpipes in the evening while we children played from waking till sleeping.

Our Wyndham house was one of a row of houses with gardens at the back adjoining the gardens of the houses in the next parallel street, and the railway line at one end and the paddock by the railway line where our new cow, a golden Jersey named Beauty, was to graze with her new black and white heifer calf, which we called Pansy. We had a fowlhouse, too, with white leghorns with bright, floppy combs and a rooster with a tall, arched tail with the end feathers arranged like a hand of playing cards.

In my memory Ferry Street and the street at the end with the shops and the office of the newspaper, *The Wyndham Farmer*, were the only streets in Wyndham. Other landmarks were the railway line and the railway station, the school, the racecourse, the golf course, and the rivers, some near, some more distant, which became as familiar to us as the rivers and paddocks and plants and trees of the other places where we had lived: the Outram Lee Stream and the Outram Glen, the brown Mimihau, the swift Mataura.

And because, in a tally of people I had known, those of fiction (and of the past and distance that transformed them into a kind of fiction – ancestors, relatives, rulers, Eliza, Simon Legree, Jack Frost, the Gypsies, Wee Willie Winkie, The Babes in the Wood, bogies and pixies and fairies) and the people in songs and in fantasy exceeded those of flesh and blood, I thought of Ferry Street as a place of mysterious people who might appear in the flesh or just as readily in poems and songs. For instance, the Murphys' house several doors away on the opposite shady side of the road with its high macrocarpa hedge, neat lawn, and moss-covered stone doorstep was the house in the song Dad sang in the evening: 'The stone outside Dan Murphy's door.' I knew he was singing of that house and the moss-covered stone, and I'd peep through the hand hole in the gate or a gap in the macrocarpa hedge and stare and stare at the 'stone outside Dan Murphy's door,' materialized from a *song*. I was filled with sadness and a peaceful feeling of belonging, for I felt that our family, too, was gathered into the song, and when Dad sang with such certainty:

> Those friends and companions of childhood,
> contented although we were poor;
> and the songs that we sung
> in the days we were young
> on the stone outside Dan Murphy's door.

I knew he was singing about us. I believed that most or all of the songs our mother and father sang referred to our life and places they had known.

> East Side West Side all around the town,
> the girls play ring-a-rosie,
> London Bridge is Falling down
> Girls and Boys together
> me and Mamie O'Rourke
> trip the light fantastic
> on the sidewalks of New York.

That was our place, too. I felt that I had been there, that it was another way of having a place without having to leave it.

And there were the sad songs about hanging men and women at the wearing of the green and the mournful bagpipe melodies that spiraled and shirrgled and moaned up into the sky; and the war songs that Dad began to sing – Tipperary, Blightie, Mademoiselle from Armentières – and the one which wrung our hearts with pity for him and the other soldiers, 'Oh, my, I don't want to die/I want to go home.'

There were the 'new' songs, too, which suddenly everyone was singing, sometimes as if with a touch of daring, 'Moonlight and Roses,' 'It ain't no sense sitting on the fence all by yourself in the moonlight,' which even then we children knew as 'It ain't no fun sitting on your bum all by yourself in the moonlight.' There was 'Tiptoe through the tulips,' 'Hello Hello Who's Your Lady Friend,' which was now Isabel's or, as we called her, *Dots'* song – 'Hello Hello who's your lady friend / who's the little girlie by *nor tide*,' she sang. And the forbidden song 'Hallelulia I'm a bum, Hallelulia bum again . . .'

And there was Dad's special song, which he sang to Mum. They'd kiss and laugh together, and Mum would blush and smile and say, 'Oh, Curly' or 'Oh, Sammy':

> Come for a trip in my airship
> come for a sail midst the stars
> come for a trip around Venus,
> come for a trip arond Mars.
> No one to watch while we're kissing,
> no one to see while we spoon,
> come for a trip in my airship
> and we'll visit the man in the moon.

And from that song, Dad would start the one which began, 'Underneath the gaslight's glitter / stands a little orphan girl,' and our hearts would swell with the sadness of knowing about the little orphan girl and with the warmth of having a mother and father and a house to live in and cows and hens and the baby rabbit found in the paddock.

Those Wyndham days were full of activity for our mother and father. Dad began painting pictures in oil on canvas and on velvet; he played us to sleep each evening with his bagpipes; he played football, breaking his ankle, which meant more time for painting the pictures. He played golf and dressed in plus fours, and one of our absorbing occupations became the unraveling of old (and sometimes new) golf balls to find what lay at the end of the crinkled thread of twangy, smelly rubber. (Theseus days indeed!) Dad went to the races, too, with Johnny Walker, the railway ganger from Australia who lived over the road and who taught us to play cards. And still there were the picnics to remote beaches and rivers, traveling in the gray Lizzie Ford, stopping on the hot, dusty roads while Dad fed water to the bubbling engine; while we looked up at the sky at what appeared to be the only other living creatures in the world – the skylarks and the circling and swooping hawks.

It was then, too, that Mother began publishing her poems each week in the *Wyndham Farmer* and soon became known, with pride, as 'Lottie C. Frame, the local poet.' There was also the exciting day when Dad brought home from the local auction a chiming clock, a set of Oscar Wilde with gold dust on the edges of the pages, a gramophone with records of 'The Wee McGregor' and 'Building a Chicken House Part One.' We played the gramophone, fascinated by the way the neck containing the needle could be swiveled and 'wrung' like a dead hen's neck, and we seized the Oscar Wilde Fairy Tales but did not read them until later, in Oamaru.

When I was two months from my fourth birthday, our youngest sister, June (Phyllis Mary Eveline), was born. That winter, like the winter in the railway huts, is remembered as miserable yet with the misery shared and banished by the way in which, instead of acting as my teasing enemies, Myrtle and Bruddie became allies against the terrible Miss Low – Miss Low, the sister of one of Dad's fishing mates, who came to look after us while the baby was born and during the first few weeks. I remember her as a tall, thin woman wearing a brown costume and spectacles with thin gold rims. Her face was unfriendly, her manner bossy: she disapproved of us. 'Lottie is too soft with them,' she said, speaking of Mother, beginning a refrain that was to continue throughout our childhood.

An evident believer in 'inner cleanliness,' she gave us regular doses of castor oil from the hated slim, blue glass bottle. And although we stayed in the house, we were forbidden to go near the front room where the baby was born and where Mother and the baby were now sleeping. Therefore we turned our misery to delight by huddling together, telling 'Miss Low' stories, lurid tales of 'the time Miss Low fell over the cliff and was killed,' 'the time Miss

Low was struck by lightning,' or drowned in a tidal wave, lost in the bush, starved in the desert, killed falling down a disused mine shaft (the English children in the comic cuts, which we were beginning to read, had many injuries falling down disused mine shafts). We rivaled each other in imagining a doom for Miss Low. 'Let's have a Miss Low story,' we'd say, snuggling together, deliciously yet miserably aware of our role as outcasts in our own home with a stranger trying to take the place of our mother.

Long after Miss Low had gone and Mum, looking after the new baby, Phyllis Mary Eveline (after Miss Low) June, whom we called Chicks, was in her ordinary place again, we continued to tell our Miss Low stories until one day, suddenly, we looked at one another, almost in embarrassment, with a sense of falseness, for we knew our need had ceased, we were happy again, and our Miss Low stories were past. We separated then, each to ourselves, focusing our attention on the new baby and on the white leghorns in the fowlhouse. We became preoccupied with the hens, wrapping them in pieces of blanket, carrying them around in our arms, giving them 'make-a-betters' (our word for *enema*, the peculiar orange-red bulbous rubber with the poky end that Mother stuck up our behinds when we wanted to go and couldn't or hadn't 'been'). For the hens we used lengths of straw. Then we'd tuck them into boxes while they, extraordinarily compliant when I think of the liberties we took with them, simply lay there, all blanketed, looking at us with their nearest eye, now and again shuttering down its white, crinkled lid over the bright steady gaze and letting out a muffled squawk.

Wyndham was the time of cabbages in the garden, of pumpwater, of candles and kerosene lamps at night with 'real' darkness and night shadows, the people in the twilight seen as if striding across the surface of the world, and at noon, standing in small people-clumps. I learned to think of everything as sharing its life and its place with a shadow; and when the candles were lit at night, Mother used to say, 'I have a little shadow that goes in and out with me.' Wyndham was also the time of other people, of neighbors whose back garden faced ours, the Bedfords with their children, Joy, Marjorie, Ronnie, each memorable for different reasons – Joy had tuberculosis, or TB, and was a patient in a sanitorium, *Waipiata*, a dreaded word in our lives. 'She's in Waipiata.' Marjorie had a 'thin little chest.' (Mother's judgment was spoken with contempt and sorrow. Every milking time she delivered a billy of milk to the Bedfords in the hope that the children would grow as 'sturdy' as we were.) Ronnie, the youngest, became famous for having stuck a bead up his nose . . .

Opposite us were the Miles, Tommy Miles and his wife and family, whom we did not know for long, for Tommy Miles, a railway ganger, was run over by the express train on the railway line outside our place. His legs were severed, and he later died in Invercargill Hospital where, in the awful language of emergency, remembered from the time the Jersey bull 'gored' Mr Bennett, he was 'rushed.' In that accident people tore up sheets to use as bandages, and Mother used what we learned to call her 'earth-quake-and-tidal-wave-voice,' announcing with high-pitched urgency, 'It's Tommy Miles, it's Tommy Miles.'

And Wyndham was the time of the dentist and starting school and Grandma Frame's dying: all three memorably unhappy, although Grandma Frame's death was different in being world-sad with everyone sharing – the cows, the hens, the pet rabbit, even the stinky ferret as well as the family and relations – while going to the dentist and starting school were miseries that belonged only to me.

The visit to the dentist marked the end of my infancy and my introduction to a threatening world of contradictions where spoken and written words assumed a special power.

One night, after Dad had 'bagpiped' us to sleep, I woke crying with a painful tooth. Dad came to where I lay in the cot, which was getting too small for me, as my feet touched the bars at the end. 'I'll tan your backside,' Dad said. His hand stung, hitting again and again on my bare bottom, and I cried again and at last fell asleep, and in the morning, faced with the inevitable teasing of Myrtle and Bruddie – 'You had a hiding last night!' – I said calmly, 'Well, I was cold anyway, and it warmed my bottom.'

I was taken to the dentist, where I kicked and struggled, thinking that something dire was about to happen to me, while the dentist, in the midst of my struggles, beckoned to the nurse, who came forward holding a pretty pink towel. 'Smell the pretty pink towel,' she said gently, and, unsuspecting, I leaned forward to smell, realizing too late as I felt myself going to sleep that I'd been deceived. I have never forgotten that deception and my amazed disbelief that I could have been so betrayed, that the words

'Smell the pretty pink towel,' without any hint of anything fearful happening, had been used to lure me into a kind of trap, that they had not *really* meant 'Smell the pretty pink towel,' but 'I'm going to put you to sleep while I take your tooth out.' How could that have been? How could a few kind words mean so much harm?

Grandma's death and burial contained none of the fury and resulting distrust of the visit to the dentist. For some time now Grandma had been in a wheelchair, and there was talk of having to amputate her other leg. I have a memory of my father coming in the door and announcing in a voice full of grief, 'The other leg's going, Mum.'

Not long after then, Grandma died, and when she was lying in the front room, Mother came to Myrtle and Bruddie and me, saying, 'Would you like to see Grandma?' The others said yes and went solemnly to look at the dead, while I hung back, afraid and always to regret that I did not see Grandma dead. When Myrtle came out of the room, I could see in her face the power of having looked at the dead.

'What was Grandma like?' I asked her, unhappily aware of the low status of second-hand experience and of my weakness at not being able to 'look.' Myrtle shrugged. 'She looked all right, just like being asleep.' For many years after that Myrtle was able to win many arguments with her triumphant 'I saw Grandma dead.' And some years later when Myrtle herself was lying dead in her coffin in the front room at Oamaru and Mother asked me, 'Do you want to see Myrtle?' I, never learning, still fearful, refused to look on the face of the dead.

Persuaded by one or two indiscretions, I was learning a measure of deceit. One day, after I'd been to the dumpy and looked down at it, at my big lots, comparing them with the baby's mess in her nappies, I saw little white things wriggling in the brown.

'Mum,' I said, 'there are little white things wriggling in it.' The alarm in Mother's face was frightening.

'Worms!' she exclaimed in horror. 'The child has worms.' That night at tea she told Dad, 'Nini has worms.'

I felt the disgrace of it. I resolved to keep my mouth shut in future.

Then, on one of our picnics, I again made a false judgment of what I should or should not say. Playing by myself in the paddock, I saw a sheep staring at me, in a special way, with its head on one side and its face full of meaning. I ran excitedly to where Mum and Dad were drinking their billy tea.

'A sheep looked at me,' I said, feeling the occasion had been momentous. I was aware that they were 'humoring' me.

'How did the sheep look at you?' Dad asked.

'With its head on one side.'

'Show us.'

Suddenly shy, with everyone staring, and sensing the ridicule, I refused; then, in a wave of (unconscious) generosity, unaware that I was creating an occasion that would be used for years to come, I said, 'I'll show only Dad.' I went to Dad, and shielding my face with my hand, I imitated the sheep's expression. Throughout my childhood Dad would say, 'Show us how the sheep looked at you,' and while the others giggled, I performed my 'routine.'

A certain wariness, a cynicism about the ways of people and of my family, and an ability to deceive, flowered fully a few months later, when on my fifth birthday I began attending Wyndham District High School, where Myrtle and Bruddie were already pupils.

6

Hark Hark the Dogs Do Bark

One morning, during my first week at school, I sneaked into Mum and Dad's bedroom, opened the top drawer of the duchesse, where the coins 'brought back from the war' were kept, and helped myself to a handful. I then went to Dad's best trousers hanging behind the door, put my hand in the pocket (how cold and slippery the lining!), and took out two coins. Hearing someone coming, I hastily thrust the money under the duchesse and left the room, and later, when the coast was clear, I retrieved my hoard and on my way to school stopped at Heath's store to buy some chewing gum.

Mr Heath looked sternly at me. 'This money won't buy anything,' he said. 'It's Egyptian.'

'I know,' I lied. Then, handing him the money from Dad's pocket, I asked, 'Will this buy me some chewing gum?'

'That's better,' he said, returning yet another of the coins, a farthing.

Armed with a supply of chewing gum, I waited at the door of the Infant Room, a large room with a platform or stage at one end and double doors opening on to Standard One, and as the children went into the room, I gave each a 'pillow' of chewing gum. Later, Miss Botting, a woman in a blue costume the same color as the castor-oil bottle, suddenly stopped her teaching and asked, 'Billy Delamare, what are you eating?'

'Chewing gum, Miss Botting.'

'Where did you get it?'

'From Jean Frame, Miss Botting.' (I was known at school as Jean and at home as Nini.)

'Dids McIvor, where did you get your chewing gum?'

'From Jean Frame, Miss.'

'Jean Frame, where did you get the chewing gum?'

'From Heath's, Miss Botting.'

'Where did you get the money?'

'My father gave it to me.'

Evidently Miss Botting did not believe me. Suddenly she was determined to get 'the truth' out of me. She repeated her question. 'Where did you get the money? I want the *truth*.'

I repeated my answer, substituting *Dad* for *father*.

'Come out here.'

I came out in front of the class.

'Go up on the platform.'

I went up on to the platform.

'Now tell me where you got the money.'

Determinedly I repeated my answer.

Playtime came. The rest of the class went out to play while Miss Botting and I grimly faced each other.

'Tell me the truth,' she said.

I replied, 'Dad gave me the money.'

She sent for Myrtle and Bruddie, who informed her with piping innocence that Dad did not give me the money.

'Yes, he did,' I insisted. 'He called me back when you had both gone to school.'

'He didn't.'

'He did.'

All morning I stayed on the platform. The class continued their reading lessons. I stayed on the platform through lunchtime and into the afternoon, still refusing to confess. I was beginning to feel afraid, instead of defiant, as if I hadn't a friend in the world, and because I knew that Myrtle and Bruddie would 'tell' as soon as they got home, I felt that I never wanted to go home. All the places I had found – the birch log in Glenham, the top of the climbers in Edendale, the places in the songs and poems – seemed to have vanished, leaving me with no place. I held out obstinately until mid-afternoon, when the light was growing thin with masses of dark tiredness showing behind it, and the schoolroom was filled with a nowhere dust, and a small voice answered from the scared me in answer to Miss Botting's repeated question: 'I took the money out of my father's pocket.'

While I'd been lying, I had somehow protected myself; I knew now that I had no protection. I'd been found out as a thief. I was so appalled by my future prospects that I don't remember if Miss Botting strapped me. I know she gave the news to the class, and it spread quickly around the school that I was a thief. Loitering at the school gate, wondering where to go and what to do, I saw Myrtle and Bruddie, carefree as ever, on their way home. I walked slowly along the cocksfoot-bordered road. I don't know when I had learned to read, but I had read and knew the stories in the primer books, and I thought of the story of the fox that sprang out from the side of the road and swallowed the child. No one knew what had happened or where the child had gone, until one day when the fox was walking by, a kind person heard, 'Let me out, let me out!' coming from the fox's belly, whereupon the kind person killed the fox, slit the belly open, and lo, the child emerged whole, unharmed, and was taken by the kind person to live in a wood in a cottage made of coconut ice with a licorice chimney . . .

I finally arrived at our place. Myrtle was leaning over the gate. 'Dad knows,' she said, in a matter-of-fact voice. I went up the path. The front door was open and Dad was waiting with the strap in his hand. 'Come into the bedroom,' he said sternly. He administered his usual 'hiding,' not excessive, as some children had, but sharp and full of anger that one of his children was a *thief. Thief, thief.* At home and at school I was now called *Thief.*

Another event that followed swiftly upon my stealing of four-pence and a handful of Egyptian coins and a farthing stays in my mind because even then I knew it to be a rich comment on the ways of the world. I was learning fast.

Margaret Cushen, the headmaster's daughter, with all the prestige attached to such a position, had a birthday. Miss Botting (still wearing the color of the castor-oil bottle and linked in my mind with the bluebottle blowflies), announcing Margaret's birthday, asked her to stand on the platform while we sang 'Happy Birthday to You.'

Then Miss Botting gave Margaret an envelope. 'It's a present from your father. Open it, Margaret.'

Margaret, flushed and proud, opened the envelope and withdrew a piece of paper that she held up for all to see. 'It's a pound note,' she said with astonished joy.

The class echoed, 'A pound note.'

'Now isn't Margaret a lucky girl to get a pound note from her father for her birthday?' Miss Botting appeared to be as excited and pleased as Margaret who, still waving her pound note, returned to her seat, stared at with awe, envy, and admiration by the rest of the class.

This sudden introduction to variations of treasure was more than I could comprehend; it is doubtful whether I had any clear thoughts about it; I had only confused feelings, wondering how money brought home from the war and clearly treasured could buy nothing, how a threepence and a penny were looked on by everyone as a fortune, and I as the thief of the fortune; yet people, especially fathers, gave their daughters pound notes for their birthdays, as if pound notes were both more and less valuable than fourpence. I wondered, too, about Miss Botting and why she had needed to keep me nearly all day on the stage, waiting for me to confess.

It happened that my new place as a school pupil who was also a known thief coincided in its inklings of the unfairness, the injustice of the world, with a changed mood of the outside world, even of our Ferry Street Wyndham. There were now more swaggers passing down Ferry Street and more coming to ask for food, they being confused in my mind with the rhyme,

> Hark hark the dogs do bark
> the beggars are coming to town.
> Some in rags, some in bags,
> and some in velvet gown.

The rhyme haunted me. I thought of the fate of the beggars and swaggers, most of whom were said to be thieves, and at night when the candles and lamps were burning I'd look out into dark Ferry Street, which was disturbed at night only by the night man with his night cart going his rounds, and I'd think of the beggars and swaggers in rags and bags and 'beastie dress' velvet, pursued by the barking dogs. I had been impressed, too, by the tales Mother told us in our Sunday Bible reading when we sat around the big kitchen table and pored over the red-letter Bible while she explained that a poor man might come to the door and be refused food or even have the dogs 'sooled' on to him, and lo! he would turn out to be an angel in disguise or even Christ himself. Mother warned us to be careful and not to laugh at people whom we thought were strange or 'funny' because they, too, might be angels in disguise. One never knew; the world was full of people in disguise, and only God knew whether or not there was an angel inside a beggar or swagger, and even if an angel were not there, God still loved each one, no matter how poor or peculiar he might be.

Nevertheless, the increasing number of swaggers passing through Wyndham and the horror and fear in people's voices when they talked of them brought a feeling of doom, of loneliness, as if something were happening or about to happen that would belong not only to us, the Frames of Ferry Street, Wyndham, but also would be part of the street and the neighbors and the other towns. Yet, literal as ever, I puzzled over the reference to some of the beggars in 'velvet gown,' for I knew that velvet was the cloth of kings and queens as well as, in my experience, the coat of beasties in the paddocks. So what secret riches did the beggars and swaggers possess?

Mother, as usual, knew the answer; they were the riches of the kingdom. 'The kingdom?' 'The kingdom of the Lord, Nini.'

It may have been heavenly intervention; it was at least blessed for me and my reputation as a thief, that we, the railway family, were now transferred from Wyndham to a town called Oamaru in the north of Otago.

7

56 Eden Street Oamaru

The long train journey is remembered as a dream of strangeness and strange landscapes: a rocketing over countless railway bridges, past swamps of flax with their tall black-beaked flax flowers, clumps of willows, the towns, their names borne along within the rhythm and the sound of the train – Clinton, Kaitangata, Milton, Balclutha – each a cluster of houses around its railway-colored railway station. I had reason indeed to believe that the world belonged to my railway father, that he was in charge of it, directing it through its miles and miles of railway lines.

I was very sick on the train, and in my half-delirious train-sick sleep, when the train changed direction, emerging from Southland toward the coast, I felt we were returning to Wyndham, and throughout the remainder of the journey I could not determine the 'right' direction, and my head whirled as I tried to work out our place in north, south, east, and west. I lay covered with a coat, on a double seat in the carriage, listening to the sound of the wheels on the rails and the voice of the guard as we approached each station and the sound of the name of the station and the clang clang of the crossing bells – ting ting, Clinton Clinton, Inch Clutha, Balclutha, Kaitangata Kaitangata. Kaitangata pursuing us when we had left it miles away, returning to us. Clinton Clinton. We passed over turbulent rivers, hodda-hodda on the wooden bridges; a desolate landscape of more swamps, flax, rushes, willows, all the kin of water.

We came to Lake Waihola. Someone said that Lake Waihola reached as far as the center of the earth, it was fathomless, and I looked out of the carriage window while Mother in her indelible voice of mystery and wonder said, 'Lake Waihola, kiddies, Lake Waihola.'

We arrived at Caversham, where I was brought abruptly into my immediate past, for although Aunty Han (whom I thought of as

Aunty *Ham*) and Uncle Bob, the baker, lived at Caversham, the chief landmark for me was the industrial school, which had been mentioned when I was 'found out' as a thief. 'We'll have you sent to the industrial school at Caversham.' It was Dad's favorite threat to Myrtle, too, when she was disobedient. I could not see the industrial school from the train. I did not know precisely what it was, but I had a picture of a school covered with dust in colors of punishment brown.

On our first night in Oamaru, we stayed with Aunty Mima (whom we thought of as Aunty *Miner*) and Uncle Alex, the taxi driver, on Wharf Street on the South Hill, and the next morning we went to where we were to live for the next fourteen years: Fifty-six Eden Street, Oamaru.

Seeing the long street and the rows of houses, especially the houses overlooking and surrounding us, Mother panicked, speaking in her earthquake-and-lightning voice. 'We've never been sur-rounded by houses before,' she said, as if the fact were a national and world disaster that caused us, too, to sense the enormity of Oamaru, where houses and people and streets replaced our familiar landscape of wild spaces, Southland skies with their shimmerings of Antarctic ice, paddocks of cattle and sheep, dark swamps, brown rivers, where each day and night could be felt in its existence, and the grass and the insects in the grass could speak and be heard.

We'd had to say good-bye to our cows, Beauty and Pansy, who'd gone to the sale yards. And Dad had 'given up' the Lizzie Ford. The Great Depression had begun.

We were to be real town dwellers with electric lights and a pull-the-chain lavatory instead of a dumpy hole, and at first the rush of water frightened us, and the brightly lit rooms with the furniture deprived of its big enveloping shadows seemed harsh and too public. We were to have town milk, delivered each morning, and Dad was to ride a bicycle to work. And stricken though we children were at such change, once we had recovered from the train journey, we were overjoyed at the house and the land and the hill of pine plantations at the back, a town reserve, separated from us by the inevitable 'bull paddock,' with a creek from the reservoir flowing through it. There were new streets and street names, new trees, new people. And the sea. And a new school.

And coinciding dramatically with our life's upheaval, some months later there was the Napier earthquake with the news and the description being given full disaster treatment by Mother's voice as she stood in the light of our new dining-room window, in front of the silver-scrolled, brown-polished Singer sewing machine (daring the lightning to strike) and talked of the Napier earthquake. The dining room was the large middle room with the big rectangular sash window (with its heavy pulleys and cords that we children soon snapped in our energetic climbing in and out), the only source of light in the room. In moments of family importance, Mother formed the habit of standing by that window, placing her feelings, like trophies, to be revealed and illuminated. That dining room held the 'king's' sofa and the king's chairs and one or two items bought at the Wyndham auction rooms. It was used only on special occasions, for visitors and for feasts like Christmas and the New Year with its first-footing and for the announcement of family and national and world triumphs and disasters.

At the back of the house, next to the dining room, there was a kitchen with a coal range and a coal bin, which was used as a seat beside the fire. Beyond the kitchen was the back bedroom, its wallpaper patterned with small, pink roses, where Grandad Frame, who was now to live with us, was to sleep. The other door from the kitchen led to the scullery with the sink (and the cockroaches beneath it), while the scullery door led down five or six wooden steps to the backyard, with the washhouse at the right, with the copper and the copper fire, the tubs and the cracked window. Toward the coal house, at one end of the washhouse, was the lavatory with a shelf for a candle, as there was no electric light in the washhouse; with the lavatory door opening toward a dark spider-haunted 'under the house.'

The other door from the dining room led to the front passage with a bathroom at one end, with a real bath and shower and hot and cold water running from taps, and a front door at the other end; with three bedrooms leading from the passage – one nearest the bathroom, where Myrtle, Isabel, June, and I were to sleep in the big double bed with the brass ends; one bedroom at the front where Bruddie was to sleep; and the room opposite, with the other double bed and the duchesse and the mirrored wardrobe, which was for Mum and Dad.

At the back of the house, outside, there was another opening to 'under the house,' which we learned to call the cellar, where we played on wet days and from where we explored 'under the house.'

There were fruit trees in the back garden – a winter pear and a honey pear growing on one tree, a plum tree belonging to the neighbors but leaning into our place, an Irish Peach apple tree, a cooking apple tree, an apricot tree, and gooseberries and black-currants. In front there was a flower garden bordering the lawn with a rose arch in one corner of the lawn, behind the high African thorn hedge, and at the side, near our parents' bedroom and beside the macrocarpa hedge, separating us from the McMurtries next door, was a summerhouse, covered with small cream banksia roses (which we called bankshee roses), which we came to use as a playhouse and theater. The hedge on the other side of the section was holly, while the back hedge between us and the bull paddock was African thorn.

As soon as we arrived at Fifty-six Eden Street, Oamaru, we children began crawling and climbing everywhere, over every inch of the red-painted iron roof, along every earthy space between the piles under the house. We noted the inhabitants with whom we were to share our life: the insects, bees, mason bees, night bees, butterflies, grandfather moths, spiders, red spiders, furry spiders, trapdoor spiders; the birds, flocks of goldfinches, wax-eyes, black-birds, sparrows, starlings. We found cat skeletons under the house and sheep and cattle skeletons in the long grass of the bull paddock, where there was no longer a bull, only, from time to time, a group of young, skittering steers. We discovered every climbable place in the hedges and trees and on the summerhouse, accumulating our treasure of new experiences, which soon included the neighbors on each side and across the road, and beyond the bull paddock to the hill with its caves and fossilized shells, the zigzag with its native plants and the seat at the top with the plaque 'Donated by the Oamaru Beautifying Society'; and the pine plantations, to be known as the 'plannies': the first one harmless, where you could look through to daylight beyond, the second frightening with the trees so densely packed that halfway through it you found yourself in a brown pine-needle darkness and knew there was no turning back, the third planny, small and full of daylight, the fourth, of stripling gums leading into pines extending down the hill at the end of Glen Street Gully, near the 'orchard,' which, because it appeared to stand alone, independent of any house or person, we believed to be ownerless and therefore, in the 'finds keeps' tradition, belonging to us.

We soon learned to know the creek, too, in its every change of flow regulated by the water in the reservoir. We knew the plants on its banks and in the creek the rocks, cockabullies, eels, and the old weighted shredded sacks of drowned kittens and cats. Each morning we set out foraging for experience and in the afternoon returned to share with one another, while our parents, apart from us now, went about their endless adult work, which might better have been known as 'toil' in all its meanings – trap or snare, battle, strife, a spell of severe, fatiguing labor – meanings of which we were unaware. Dad worked all day, and sometimes, on night shift, all night, sleeping during the day, while we, the railway children, vanished into the pine plannies or along Glen Street Gully to our orchard or crept stealthily about the summerhouse, 'Sh-sh, Dad's asleep . . .'

All except June or Chicks attended the Oamaru North School, where I was in Standard One, Miss Carroll's class. I remember little of her except that she strapped me once for talking and her face was curved with the teeth scarcely contained and her mouth seeming scarcely able to close over her teeth to prevent them from flying out. More important in my memory is the walk between home and school, the various streets and houses and gardens, the blossoming trees lining the streets, the animals I met, the exciting sense of the structure of the new town with its town clock, chiming every quarter-hour, visible from that one spot on our way to school – the corner of Reed and Eden Street by Hunt's red corrugated iron fence. Here, as nine o'clock in the morning approached, we checked our earliness or lateness, using as a second reference a small, lame woman, with one shortened leg encased in a thick, black boot who passed the corner at ten to nine sharp each morning and became known to us as the Late Lady, for seeing her meant that to avoid being late, we'd have to run the rest of the way to school. It was the tradition, however, to walk to and from school in the morning and afternoon but to run home for lunch, partly because the lunch-hour was short and home was halfway up Eden Street. Having just turned seven I accepted this tradition without question, as I accepted all the traditions of the Oamaru North School. I ran home for lunch each day, stopping only at Mrs Feather's corner store to collect the freshly baked sandwich loaf, which I carefully picked at on the 'mounted' side to level it. The big boys of Eden Street, running faster than I and with still further to go, wheeled, leaning around Hunt's Corner, using their bodies like machines, and as they passed me, one would hiss in my ear, 'I'm after you,' an announcement which, I soon learned, was to be accepted with a mixture of pride and fear and told to others in a voice that held a hint of 'skiting' – 'One of the big boys is after me.'

Life at Oamaru with all its variety of new experiences was a wonderful adventure. I was now vividly aware of myself as a person on earth, feeling a kinship with other creatures and full of joy at the sights and sounds about me and drunk with the anticipation of play, where playing seemed endless, on and on after school until dark, when even then there were games to play in bed – physical games like 'trolley works' and 'fitting in,' where each body curled into the other and all turned on command, or guessing games or imagining games, interpreting the masses of shape and color in the bedroom curtains, or codes, hiding messages in the brass bed knobs. There were arguments and fights and plans for the future and impossible dreams of fame as dancers, violinists, pianists, artists.

That year I discovered the word *Island*, which in spite of all teaching I insisted on calling Is-Land. In our silent reading class at school, when we chose one of the Whitcombes school readers, those thin, fawn-covered books with crude drawings on the cover and speckled pages, I found a story, *To the Island*, an adventure story that impressed me so much that I talked about it at home.

'I read a story, *To the Is-Land*, about some children going to an Is-Land.'

'It's I-Land,' Myrtle corrected.

'It's not,' I said. 'It's Is-Land. It says,' I spelled the letters, 'I-s-l-a-n-d. Is-land.'

'It's a silent letter,' Myrtle said. 'Like knee.'

In the end, reluctantly, I had to accept the ruling, although within myself I still thought of it as the Is-Land.

I began reading more 'adventure' books, realizing that to have an adventure, I did not need to travel in the lost Lizzie Ford, getting sick on the way, to beaches and rivers – I could experience an adventure by reading a book. And, as usual, being eager to share my discovery, I told the family about my new way of having adventures, instantly regretting my indiscretion, for whenever Mum or Dad saw me curled up on the coal bin with a book, they'd say in that humiliatingly knowing way, 'Have you come to the adventure yet?'

This concentration on adventures that to me meant simply amazing escapes from physical danger, rescues, being lost and found, triumphing in disaster, was increased by the teacher's repeated order for the class to write a composition, 'My Adventure.' It never occurred to me that I was allowed to make up an adventure, like a story. I mourned my apparent lack of adventures as I heard those of other children being read out to the class – visits to remote towns, museums, zoos. My staple adventure was crossing the bull paddock, where there was not even a bull, only a bunch of steers, and finding my way through the second 'planny' beyond the point of darkness when my heart began to beat fast and the green world was lost in the dark trees and the deep drifts of fallen pine needles, some many feet deep over the entrances to old rabbit warrens; but I felt shy of disclosing that adventure because it was different from that of the others in the class where the insistence was on the escapes, broken limbs, runaway horses . . .

My reading was limited to schoolbooks, including the school journal, and the new comic cuts, which we were sometimes allowed to buy from Mr Adams – My Favorite, Rainbow, Tiger Tim, Chick's Own, with the best which Myrtle and I read being My Favorite because the print was smaller and there were therefore more stories, and Rainbow. Bruddie's comic was Tiger Tim, and Dots and Chicks had Chick's Own. An attraction of My Favorite was *Terry and Trixie of the Circus*, who inspired our current ambition to be trapeze artists, particularly as the song, The Daring Young Man on the Flying Trapeze, was also in vogue.

Much of the school journal dealt with celebrations of the British Empire, with articles and photographs of the royal family, chiefly the two little princesses, Elizabeth and Margaret Rose. There was a description, too, of their life-size dolls' house, with photographs. In contrast to the factual prose of the school journal and the praise of the Empire, the king, the governor general, the Anzacs at Gallipoli, Robert Falcon Scott at the South Pole, the poems were full of mystery and wonder, with Walter de la Mare and John Drinkwater, Christina Rossetti, as the editor's first choices followed by Alfred Noyes and John Masefield, to give the rollicking touch. One poem that I liked at once was 'Meg Merrilees.' Gypsies, beggars, robbers, swaggers, slaves, thieves, all the outcast victims of misfortune who yet might be angels in disguise, had become part of my dreams and comprehension of the Outside World. I learned by heart 'Old Meg she was a gypsy . . .,' and again, sharing my discovery at home by reciting it to the family, I was urged again and again to repeat it, and when I'd oblige and each time came to the line 'And 'stead of supper she would stare/Full hard against the moon,' everyone would laugh, apparently at my earnestness, or perhaps because there was seldom any question that I, with known 'hollow legs' and the habit of devouring slice after slice of 'bread 'n' golden syrup,' would ever have to stare at the moon instead of enjoying my supper.

When I thought of Old Meg, I felt the sadness that came with the way the words went in the poem, the same way the words went in the songs about Glasgow and the sidewalks of New York and the streets of Dublin, 'Dublin's fair city . . .' I pictured Old Meg as like Ma Sparks – I thought Ma Sparks and Old Meg might have been the same person – who everyone said was a gypsy the way she squatted at the top of her path outside her front door in Glen Street and stared down at the street and the small unofficial rubbish dump the other side of the street, into the bull paddock, and across the hill where the pigeons, kept by several people in Glen Street, were out for their evening flight, circling the hill, the plantations, and the town with a sudden rush of wings over our house.

Ma smoked a pipe. They said she wore no pants, and you could see if you walked along Glen Street and looked up at her squatting there.

Beside the word *adventure*, other words began to appear repeatedly in our learning and written expression, and although they were not, I felt, attractive words, they had a dramatic effect in their use. I remember learning to spell and use these three words: *decide*, *destination*, and *observation*, all of which worked closely with *adventure*. I was enthralled by their meaning and by the fact that all three seemed to be part of the construction of every story – everyone was *deciding*, having a *destination*, *observing* in order to decide and define the destination and know how to deal with the *adventures* along the way. Partly as a result of the constant coming and going of our relatives and of our own shifting from place to place, I had an exaggerated sense of movement and change, and when I found I could use this necessary movement to create or notice adventures, I was overjoyed. Our teacher introduced lessons in observation, where we were instructed to make a habit of 'observing' on our walk to and from school, and once again it was this walk that gave me a fund of instruction. I had several choices of route (I could *decide* for myself), which I learned to vary. The 'ordinary' journey took me down Eden Street, past Hunt's corner (and the Kearns' Alsatian dogs) into Reed Street, the cherry blossom street, and along Reed Street to the North School. Reed Street was a 'doctors' street with Dr Orbell, our doctor, a teasing old man who frightened us with his jokes, living in his two-storied house near the corner, while further along the street, occupying a whole block, the garden walled like Buckingham Palace, the Smith-Mortons lived and near them the Fitzgeralds, in their two-storied houses. The doctors' daughters had names like *Adair* and *Geraldine*, and they did not go to our school, but to boarding schools in another town in the North Island (Is-Land). They had dolls' houses, too, and ponies, Shetland ponies, and they 'learned' things, such as dancing, music, elocution. (To 'learn' something was the dream of our lives.)

Or I could walk to school up Aln Street, a narrow earth street always in shade, with a formidable high clay bank on one side with water always running down the bank and across the road. The expanse of yellow clay was more like a creature than earth, the way it leaned up against the hill. It was excitingly unformed, and I used to stand looking up at it half with interest, half with fear, and one day, as I stood staring in Aln Street, a woman came by. 'Hello, little girl,' she said. 'Here's two shillings.' With much wonder I took the two shillings. I didn't go to school that day. Instead, I returned to Mrs Feather's store, where I bought a shilling's worth of acid drops and a shilling's worth of chlorydne lollies (a cough lolly containing chloroform, although I did not know this) and walked around the streets, eating my lollies, until it was after-school time, when I came home and fell asleep for eighteen hours, and when I woke I was violently sick. 'What happened?' Mum asked. 'A lady gave me two shillings,' I said.

Sometimes my walk took me, daringly, the length of Eden Street, past the Church of Christ near the corner, with its Wayside Pulpit Thought for the Week, which I read carefully, taking literally the shortened parables about shepherds, sheep, and sinners. If I went a little out of my way, I could stare at Fraser's Bacon Factory.

On my way down Eden Street I always crossed over to the garage of Dewar and McKenzies, which I thought of as *Jewel McKenzies*, to sniff the petrol smell and ask if they had a free ink blotter, for they were known to have a supply of these, and the wildfire word was about, *Jewel McKenzies have free blotters*.

Along Humber Street (which I thought of as Humble Street), I walked by the railway and the engine and goods sheds and stopped by another place that haunted me – an old stone house leaning against a deserted shop. The house was plain, the garden overgrown with dandelions and dock and daisies, with a gate in the low Oamaru stone wall opening on to a long path leading up to the front door. Yvonne Baker lived there, it was said. The house resembled her, for she was small, her skin was damp, her hair lank as if she, too, lived on the damp side of the street and had grown cold and damp like the house. There was never any sign of life, no curtains in the blank windows, but the stone house, like the clay bank in Aln Street, had the appearance of being alive in its stone and moss, and it was one of my cherished 'observations' and adventures.

My other route was along Thames Street, which had become the point of reference in light and sound in our family, with Dad saying, 'Keep your voice down. You can be heard down *Thames Street*.' Or, 'What do you think we are, all the lights in the house blazing; you can see them from *Thames Street*.' In Thames Street my chief place of call was the lolly shop with its notice *High Class Confectionery*, which I read as High *Glass* Confectionery, kept by Miss Bee and her sister, also a Miss Bee. How I puzzled over their names and their origins and the meaning and appearance of their *High Glass*!

8

Death and a Sickness

From being a horizontal thread or path that one followed or traversed, time in that year suddenly became vertical, to be ascended like a ladder into the sky with each step or happening following quickly on the other. I was not yet eight. The depression was at its height. There were beginnings, endings, gains, losses, with a large share of misery where there was no place to lay the blame; there was no help in saying, 'You're the *blame*,' or in calling anything or anyone *Thief*, for it was a world misery; it was not even God's doing, for Mother insisted that God was kind, and although everything had its purpose, God always acted to love, and not to hurt, the people in the world.

Grandad Frame was living with us. He was old and thin, and his baggy pants had a shiny behind, and he slept in the back room. His head rested, tilted, on his neck, like a bird's head, and he wore glasses with thin gold rims, which he kept in a dark blue case lined with rich blue velvet, which filled me with sadness whenever I saw it: it was a color that had no end, like the depths of the sky in the evening, and it was like the question that I had begun to ask myself, dizzying my head with the search for an answer, 'Why *was* the world, why *was* the world?' which immediately gave the thought of *no world* and a feeling of everlasting depths from which one had to struggle to escape.

In some way, Grandad's glasses case and the sound of it snipping open and shut and the fact that he left it behind when he died made it for me the essence of Grandad Frame and his life with us. As my youngest sister, June or Chicks, had not yet started school, he was her special friend, calling her his Mickey Mouse, his Iteymitie; she was so small.

Grandad was not ill, nor was he very old; he must have been tired, for he died one night in his sleep, and he was put in a coffin in the front room with the blinds pulled down so that everyone in the street knew that someone in the house had died; that was the custom: you could tell if people were dead by the pulled-down blinds, and you could tell if people were home by the smoke coming out of their chimney.

On the day of the funeral the Fletts next door looked after us, giving us scrambled eggs to eat and teaching us how to knit with big wooden knitting needles. We looked through their holly hedge at the funeral going from our place, with all the relations dressed up and speaking in their high-up voices, and it didn't seem to be our place. The aunts were there, still talking of Up Central and Middlemarch (Middlemarch, Lottie) and Inchclutha; and the uncles with their shy Frame look and the particular set of the lips that said, 'Everything should be perfect. Why isn't it?' And on Sunday, when we all went to the cemetery on the South Hill to put flowers on Grandad's grave, I was surprised to find that Grandma was buried there beside him, after dying in Wyndham, and I imagined her making that same twisty railway journey from Wyndham, past the rivers and the swamps and the small railway-colored railway stations and Lake Waihola and Caversham with the industrial school and Dunedin and Seacliff, where the loonies lived, and Hampden with the black swans and the lagoon, all the way to the South Hill, Oamaru. Grandma traveling with her black dress and her Grandma smell and her song 'Carry Me Back to Ole Virginny' and that other song for sleep and night-time, 'Shoo shaggy o'er the glen, Mama's pet and Daddy's hen . . .'

We put the flowers in their jam jar on Grandad and Grandma's grave, and we looked curiously at the tall tombstone with its list of Frame dead. There was one, Janet Frame, my name. Died aged thirteen months.

Soon the back bedroom became known as Bruddie's room instead of Grandad's room. It had no curtain because it didn't look out at houses and the street, only toward the hill and the plannies and, nearer, at the back garden and the patch of bright green grass where the tap leaked, next to the clump of dock which we valued for its flaming leaves in autumn and its green seed changing to red, from which we brewed our pretend tea. 'Do have a cup of dock-seed tea, Mrs . . .'

Grandad's death was different from Grandma's in that I did not feel that it belonged to us; it was an event that belonged to the grown-ups, who performed their duties of dressing correctly and

47

talking of Middlemarch and Up Central and the 'Outram days, Lottie and George,' and burying Grandad while we children observed from a distance, trying to distinguish between rumor and truth. Myrtle said Grandad had been nailed down so he could not escape. But how could he escape if he was dead? He could escape as a ghost, she said. But there were no ghosts. Who said? The Bible said. (We were learning to apportion prestige to the makers of rules. *The Bible said* was a convincing source, while on a more mundane level, *Dad said* usually won over *Mum said*.)

It was not long after Grandad's death that we were awakened one night by a commotion in the house. I heard Mum crying out, 'Bruddie's having a convulsion; Bruddie's having a convulsion.' I ran with the others into the dining room. We sat together on the king's sofa, watching and listening while Mum and Dad went back and forth from Bruddie's room to the bathroom. 'A convulsion, a convulsion,' Mum kept saying in her earthquake-and-tidal-wave voice. She fetched the doctor's book from where it was (unsuccessfully) hidden on top of the wardrobe in their bedroom and looked up *Convulsions*, talking it over with Dad, who was just as afraid.

In the meantime Bruddie had wakened, sobbing. 'A bath,' Mother cried. 'Put him in a bath.' Dad carried the crying Bruddie into the bathroom. We four girls were sent back to our bedroom, where we cuddled up to one another, talking in frightened whispers and shivering with the cold Oamaru night, and when I woke the next morning, my eyes were stinging with sleep and I felt burdened with the weight of a new awful knowledge that something terrible had happened in the night to Bruddie.

Our lives were changed suddenly. Our brother had epilepsy, the doctor said, prescribing large doses of bromide which, combined with Bruddie's now frequent attacks, or fits, as everyone called them, only increased his confusion and fear until each day at home there were episodes of violent rage when he attacked us or threw whatever was at hand to throw. There had usually been somewhere within the family to find a 'place' however cramped; now there seemed to be no place; a cloud of unreality and disbelief filled our home, and some of the resulting penetrating rain had the composition of real tears. Bruddie became stupefied by drugs and fits; he was either half-asleep, recovering, crying, from the last fit, or in a range of confusion that no one could understand or help. He still went to school, where some of the bigger boys began to bully him, while we girls, perhaps prompted by the same feeling of fear, tried to avoid him, for although we knew what to do should he fall in a fit at school or outside at home, we could not cope with the horror of it. Mother, resisting fiercely the advice of the doctors to put Bruddie in an institution, nursed him while we girls tried to survive on our own with the occasional help of Dad, who now combed the tangles out of my frizzy hair each morning and supervised our cleaning of our bedroom. His insistence that we sweep the 'skirting boards' gave me a new, interesting word: skirting boards. Another new word of that time was *wainscot*: 'A mouse in the *wainscot* scratches, and scratches,' from the poem 'Moonlit Apples,' by John *Drinkwater*.

After the first panic and whirlwind of having a sickness in the family and knowing there was no cure, there was a period of dullness and calm, perhaps as the rain from the cloud soaked into our bones. Bruddie left school. Mother now devoted all her time to him. Anyone observing me during those days would have seen an anxious child full of twitches and tics, standing alone in the playground at school, wearing day after day the same hand-me-down tartan skirt that was almost stiff with constant wear, for it was all I had to wear: a freckle-faced, frizzy-haired little girl who was somehow 'dirty' because the lady doctor chose her with the other known 'dirty and poor' children for a special examination in that narrow room next to the teacher's room. I had tide marks of dirt behind my knees and on my inner arms, and when I saw them, I felt a wave of shock to know they were there when I had been sure I had washed thoroughly.

Strangely enough, my consuming longing, in the midst of the shock of sickness in the family, was to be invited to join in the wonderful skipping games played by the rest of the class with brand-new, golden-knotted rope owned and controlled by one of the girls. How could a length of ordinary clothesline rope, so new it still had the hairs sticking to it, confer such power? I stood there day after day by the Oamaru stone wall, waiting and waiting for the signal to skip, 'All in together/this fine weather,' or 'Two little girls in navy blue/These are the actions they must do./Salute to the King/bow to the Queen . . .' which, however, was not so desirable as 'all in together,' for there no one had to worry about being chosen or not chosen, for it was all in together when I and the other timid children waiting could sneak in under cover and care of the game itself. Most of the time, however, the skippers were carefully chosen by those in power – The farmer wants a wife, the wife wants a child, the child wants a toy . . .

There was one other child known as 'dirty': Nora Bone, whom I despised because she, like myself, was seldom asked to join the skipping, but whose need was so strong that she always offered to 'core for ever,' that is, turn and turn the skipping rope and never herself join in the skipping. She was known as 'the girl who cores for ever.' There were only two or three in the whole school, and everyone treated them contemptuously. Nora Bone, the girl who cores for ever. There was no more demeaning role. No matter how much I longed to join in the games, I never offered to core for ever.

So Bruddie was a sick boy. The world swept on with its morning, noon, night, and the Great Depression stalked the streets and the homes of Oamaru, bringing the 'sack' and the 'dole' for many and wage cuts for my father, whose voiced fear, communicating itself to us, was of the 'sack' and 'going bankrupt,' and as the doctor and the hospital bills began to arrive, Dad would sit at the end of the table, leaning his head in his hands, and say, 'Mum, I'm going bankrupt. I'll go mad and shoot meself. I'll go down and jump over the wharf.' And Mum would reply quickly, 'None of that talk, Curly. God will help us.' 'He'd better be lively, then, and jump to it,' Dad would say, always irreverent in mentioning God and religion, which he dismissed as mumbo jumbo. Mother would say then, like a gramophone record, 'Consider the lilies of the field . . . Take no thought of the morrow.'

Something new, a silent time of deeper thinking, had entered my life, and I associate it with those afternoons of silent reading, the very name of the activity puzzling me, when the silence was so full of inner noise that I could not make myself interested in the Whitcombes Readers. We were 'on to' Pinocchio; I thought it was a stupid story. I thought Don Quixote was a fool. I sat doing nothing on those dreary afternoons, full of thinking yet not knowing what I was thinking, watching the beams of dust, whitened with chalk, floating around in the window light and knowing that I used to think they were sunbeams.

Then, one afternoon, when we had singing from the Dominion Song Book, a class I loved, we sang a haunting song, 'Like to the tide moaning in grief by the shore,/mourn I for friends captured and warriors slain . . .' We sang the Maori words, too: E pare ra . . . As we were singing, I felt suddenly that I was crying because something terrible had happened, although I could not say what it was: it was inside the song, yet outside it, with me. When school was over, I ran home, even passing some of the big boys at Hunt's Corner, and when I reached the gate, I was out of breath. I came around the corner into the back yard. Myrtle was standing there. 'The Old Cat is dead,' she said abruptly.

We buried the Old Cat in the garden. She had been black and fluffy, and when she grew old, her fur grew brown as if it had been scorched. Since we had lived in Oamaru, cats and their kittens had arrived from nowhere to live with us and there was a special place in the washhouse near the copper where they always had their kittens. Although we were never allowed to have the cats inside, we sometimes sneaked them in when Dad was at work, and we were close to them in their births and deaths. We did not then each have an animal. Myrtle's Old Cat was shared with all, and it was now unthinkable that another animal would not arrive to take the place of Old Cat.

The sad afternoon of the singing of 'E para ra' became part of my memories, like the wind in the telegraph wires and the discovery of My Place. I thought it was strange that we could be singing of 'friends captured and warriors slain' while I could be seeing in my mind the lonely beach with the tide 'moaning in grief by the shore' and people on the beach who were the people in the song, the warriors, and others who were Myrtle, Bruddie, and I at Waipapa or Fortrose; yet at the same time I could be feeling a dread and unhappiness that I could not name, which had little relation to this song, and still at the same time be sitting in the brown classroom, watching the dust traveling in and out of the beams of light slanting through the windows that were so tall that the monitors had to struggle each morning to open them, using ropes and levers and a long pole with a hook on the end; all school windows were thus, constantly at war with being opened or shut. And when Myrtle said, 'Old Cat's dead,' I knew it already; yet it was something else, too, as well as Old Cat.

About two weeks later Myrtle arrived home from school with Lassie, the spaniel dog, which had quite naturally followed her. Well, Lassie was a bitch because she was fat with rows of titties, but we were forbidden to say the word *bitch*. In spite of arguments and threats from Dad and talk of hydatids from Mum, we kept Lassie and two of the pups that were born the following week. The others were tied in a sugar bag with a stone to weigh them down and drowned in the creek. Gradually over the years, the bed of the creek became the resting place of many cats, kittens, pups, not only from us but from neighbors, with now and then, when the sack rotted, a wet cat shape with teeth set in a skeleton snarl, rising to the surface.

9
Poppy

One day I found a friend, Poppy, whose real name was Marjorie. She had lank brown hair, an ugly face with a wide red mouth, and her father whipped her with a narrow machine belt, which made cuts in her skin. Everything she said and did was new to me, even the way she talked and the words she used, her ideas and games and the folklore that I didn't think of as folklore but as truth rumors passed from one person to another. Poppy taught me how to cure warts by squeezing the juice of the ice plant over them. We'd sit on the Glen Street clay bank that was covered with purple-flowering ice plant, and we'd wriggle as the stems of the ice plant dug into our bottoms, and we'd squeeze the juice of the stems over our warts, and, miraculously, within a few days our warts disappeared. Poppy taught me how to suck the acid from the stalks of a plant she called shamrock – later I learned it was oxalis – and we'd sit, enjoying the stinging taste of the acid; she taught me how to suck honey from the periwinkle flower and to eat and enjoy the sweet floury berries of the hawthorn. She explained that if we were walking to school and separated with a lamp post between us, then we 'had the pip' with each other and were not allowed to speak until we linked little fingers, a gesture that was also necessary when we both said the same word at the same time.

These new rituals delighted me. Poppy taught me how to 'cadge' flowers, too. She explained that any flower which grew through the fence onto the road could be 'cadged' and belong to us, and it wasn't stealing, for they belonged to us *by right*. Each day we'd arrive at school and home with armfuls of flowers, the names of all of which Poppy knew and taught me. We were studying grasses and weeds at school, and we were both drunk with the glory of the new names – shepherd's purse, fat hen (what a giggle!), ragwort, where the black and white caterpillars lived, though we preferred the woolly ones that turned into *Red Admirals*.

After school I used to go to Poppy's place to play school in her washhouse, where we lined up her father's empty beer bottles and made them breathe in and out, and do dry land swim with chest elevator, arms bend upward stretch, running on the spot with high knee raising. We also gave them tables and asked them to name and draw the clouds, cirrus, nimbus, stratus, cumulus, while we chanted the names, cirrus, nimbus, stratus, cumulus . . . We made them learn the mountains in the mountain chains, too – Rimutaka, Tararua, Ruahine, Kaimanawa . . . And we strapped them, saying sharply, 'Pay attention. Come out here.' The beer bottles stood in a row on the bench facing northwest, lit golden by the rays of the setting sun shining through the dusty little window. Sometimes, if we broke a bottle, we looked through a piece of glass at the golden world.

It seemed to me that Poppy knew everything. She knew the names and uses that were not the ordinary uses of everyday things. She also had a 'place' that she spoke of, where she used to go to stay with relatives at *Moeraki*. She pronounced the word as if she owned it, the way the aunts pronounced Up Central, Middlemarch, and Inch Clutha.

Then one day Poppy asked me if I would like to borrow her special book that she kept in her washhouse among a clutter of treasures in an old beer barrel. 'It's Grimm's Fairy Tales,' she said. I had never heard of such a book, but I said I'd like to borrow it. And that night I took Grimm's Fairy Tales to bed and began to read, and suddenly the world of living and the world of reading became linked in a way I had not noticed before. 'Listen to this,' I said to Myrtle and Dots and Chicks. They listened while I read the Twelve Dancing Princesses, and as I read and they listened, I knew and they knew, gloriously, that *we* were the Dancing Princesses – not twelve but four; and as I read, I saw in my mind the place in the coat cupboard in the corner of the bedroom where we could vanish to the underground world and the orchard that was 'our' orchard along the gully where the boughs of the trees honked and cried out when they were broken, silver and gold trees; and in the end it was Myrtle who married the old soldier who, in my mind, looked like Vincent, the man of twenty-two, to us, shriveled and old, who had fallen in love with Myrtle, who was barely twelve when she went for a holiday to the Wyndham Walkers.

And the shoes, danced each morning to shreds, we knew about

those, with our own shoe soles flapping away from the uppers, and Dad sitting carefully marking and cutting the leather, and with the tacks in his mouth, bending over the bootlast while he half-soled and heeled our shoes, complaining, like the king in the story, 'Where have you been that your toes are scuffed and your soles are worn through?' Where indeed!

What a wonderful story it was – orchards hung with silver and golden apples, boughs that spoke and sang and cried out, underground seas and rivers and splash splash through the dark caverns, then suddenly the lit palace and the ballroom.

All the stories had a similar measure of delight and excitement – The Blue Light, the Juniper Tree, the old favorites from the primer reading books – Hansel and Gretel, Snow White, all the tales of Mother, Father, Sister, Brother, Aunt, Uncle, none of whom were more nor less than we were, for all the list of extraordinary gifts, miracles, transformations, cruelties, and the many long years of wandering and searching, full of hope and expectation. Grimm's Fairy Tales was everybody's story seen in a special way with something new added to the ordinary rules of observation. Even the insects and animals in the stories had speech; I'd always felt as if they had; I'd known when the sheep looked at me that it was talking to me. And when the flies from the sticky flypapers were caught in my frizzy hair and buzzed and zoomed in my ear, there was no mistaking their frantic speech.

Poppy's Grimm's Fairy Tales became a treasured book to be returned and borrowed, again and again.

Poppy had two brothers, Bob and Ted, and an elder sister, Florrie, who was soon to be married. Bob, who had left school and was working, was an aloof boy with a black patch over his forehead where he was hurt trying to ride a bicycle down the hospital hill. Rumor said that if he removed his black patch, he would die. His brother, Ted, was short and wide-mouthed like Poppy and of an age for us to tease Myrtle about him. With Florrie's approaching marriage there was much talk among us of weddings and what happened when you married, with our parents giving unsatisfactory answers to our questions.

'What did you do when you married, Mum?'

'Your father and I jumped over a broomstick.'

'And where did the babies come from?'

'From the stork who brings all babies.'

Those answers were as meaningless as the teasing answer people gave when you asked them what they were making: 'A wigwam for a goose's bridle.' Fortunately, Poppy had all the information I wanted.

'You fuck,' she said.

'Fuck?'

'The man gets on top of the woman and puts his thing in her.' She explained to me about fucking and Frenchies, which a man wore on his tool to stop a woman having babies, and how the woman had a cunt and how a man 'came' and shot spunk everywhere, and if the woman started a baby and didn't want it she drank gin to get rid of it. Poppy told me the rhyme:

> Pounds shillings and pence
> a man fell over the fence.
> He fell on a lady
> and squashed out a baby.
> Pounds shillings and pence.

She knew some Mae West stories, too. Everyone was talking about Mae West and Mae West stories, and at school now, in Silent Reading, we giggled together, changing Whitcombe and Tombs to Tit, come, and wombs . . .

Florrie married. We tin-canned her and her new husband and had a feast of fizzy drinks and cakes, and a few days later Myrtle and I and Ted and Poppy went up by the second planny, where the Council men had been cutting down some of the trees, and there, where the trees were lying, among the branches and the pine needles, Myrtle and Ted tried to 'do it' while we watched with interest, seeing Ted jiggling up and down on top of Myrtle.

This new experience pleased me, and anxious as ever to share the day's events, I said casually at the tea table that evening, 'Myrtle and Ted did it in the plannies this afternoon.'

'Did what?' Dad asked.

'Fucked, of course,' I said, quite unaware that I had said anything startling; I was merely recounting the day's events.

There was a sudden sweep of horror that touched everyone at the table, and Dad crashed his fist down, making the tea things (and us) jump. 'I forbid you,' he said, 'ever to speak to Poppy and Ted and any of that family again. As for you,' he faced Myrtle, 'come into the bedroom.'

'Mum,' he called, 'where's the belt.' Mother, who never hit us and was always afraid when Dad asked for the belt, made her plea, 'Don't hit her, Curly.'

The matter was too serious, however. Dad used the belt on Myrtle while I, terrified, and in a way to 'blame,' fled with the others outside to the summerhouse. I could not understand the sudden transformation of Mum and Dad on receiving my simple item of news. I thought it was an occasion for celebration. I genuinely thought everyone would be pleased.

While Myrtle was crying and screaming in the bedroom, Dad managed to have someone fetch a doctor, for Myrtle, although only twelve now, which was young in those days, already had her 'monthlies,' which Mum had announced by the sewing machine one morning in her disaster voice, saying, 'Myrtle's come, Myrtle's come,' which was confusing until I learned it was not 'spunk' come but 'monthlies.'

The doctor arrived and went to the bedroom to examine Myrtle. We could hear her crying. Dad's fury and fear were unforgettable. The doctor spoke sharply to Dad, saying, 'She's hysterical; she's terrified.'

That night, like the night of Bruddie's illness, effected a change in our lives.

The next morning, when I saw Poppy, I said, 'I'm not allowed to play with you or speak to you ever again.'

She replied, with a tone of equal importance, 'And I'm not allowed to speak to you either.' For Poppy also, unaware of the need for secrecy, had 'told.'

The warning from our parents was so strong, the threat of the consequences of disobedience so dire, that Poppy and I parted forever, and I spoke to her only briefly once, a few years later. I returned her Grimm's Fairy Tales, comforted by realizing that although I had returned her book, I still had many of the stories in my head, that the Twelve Dancing Princesses had their permanent home at our place. They and the Blue Light and the Juniper Tree. And in every Christmas hazelnut I could still imagine a tiny dress of gold and silver folded tightly, unfolded to life-size for me to wear. 'Shake shake hazel tree / gold and silver over me.' And down by the garden tap where the grass was greenest I could still play and drink dock-seed tea and imagine the little goat feeding on the long grass and my saying, 'Bleat goat bleat / arrive table neat,' and having eaten the feast before me, bid, 'Bleat goat bleat / depart table neat.'

Once again I was alone at school. Skipping went in and out, marbles came and went, and hopscotch was in, and I spent my time searching for smooth, round 'hoppy' stones, and I'd lie in bed at night just thinking of the hoppy stones waiting to be picked up. Dots and Chicks and I played hoppy out on the footpath, pausing now and again to shout abuse at the dolled-up young women who passed by on their high heels, 'Put a little bit more powder on your face, put a little bit more powder on your face!'

And Myrtle and I became closer friends. She was in her Proficiency Year at school, and all the talk at home was of whether she'd get her proficiency, and Dad warned her that if she didn't get it she would have to go to work at the woollen mills, where she'd have to go anyway, as he couldn't afford to let her go to senior high school. And that, of course, was if she hadn't already been sent to the industrial school at Caversham.

The next wave of alarm in the family was caused by the mounting of our grocery bill at Mrs Feather's to 100 pounds, with us having no hope of paying it. Feeling proud of having such a big bill, I told my class at school, 'My father's going bankrupt. Our bill is a hundred pounds,' and once again I was not able to understand why I should not have told about the bill. I had, in the meantime, devised my own method of shopping, going to each of the shops I passed on the way to school, asking for something that I knew the shopkeeper had to fetch from the back of the shop, and while it was being fetched, helping myself to goods on the counter, slipping them quickly under my arm and holding my arm stiffly by my side, and when the shopkeeper returned, I'd say convincingly that I didn't think Mother wanted that item after all. My usual snatch was an apple or a pear, or 'lollies.' One day, greatly daring, I tried my trick in the same shop twice, and when I returned for my second steal, the woman asked, 'Did you touch anything in the shop this morning?' Terrified, I said, 'Oh no!' 'I'll put the police after you,' she said, 'if you touch anything in this shop.' I didn't go to that shop again, and although I didn't again steal from a shop, I began to buy 'fancy biscuits' from Mrs Feather, putting them down on the bill. I'd hide them in the hedge and help myself when I wanted a chocolate biscuit, although I quickly changed my hiding place when I discovered, one damp morning, a paper bag of sodden biscuits crawling with earwigs.

Sometimes I saw Poppy going on her way to school. We'd glance at each other, ashamed and shy, and cross to the other side of the road. We both knew that obedience promised less in pain than disobedience, and we were quite resigned to our separation. We were no longer friends.

Instead of having the wonderful games and stories and rumors and cadged flowers every day, I began to collect silver paper from my stolen chocolate biscuits, smoothing out the crinkled colors and pressing the pieces into a flat yellow tobacco tin, and sometimes I'd open the tin and sit enjoying the shining colors of the silver paper.

Unfortunately, my 'fiddle' with the household accounts was discovered at the end of the month. I was punished. I gave up silver paper and my ambition of making pictures with it and acquired my own ranch and my own brand of cattle, Bar X, between the yellow japonica bush and the rose arch. And then one day I was sent to buy, honestly, both chocolate and fancy biscuits stuck together with icing, because Aunty Maggie was coming to stay.

10

OK Permanent Wave

Aunty Maggie, Dad's sister, had cancer of the throat. We were told that her throat was closing up, and when it was finally closed, she would die. We were also told that Aunty Maggie (or *Mag*, as Mum and Dad called her) was very clever at knitting and fancy-work and that we were to behave while she was visiting us and not stare at her trying to eat. We sat at the table fascinated and horrified as she put more and more of her meals aside on her plate, with an apologetic glance at Mum, 'I'm sorry, Lottie. I can't manage that.'

We also watched her knit cable stitch, a supreme accomplishment that divided the world into those who could and those who could not knit cable stitch. I heard Mum talking to Mrs Walsh over the fence, 'Dad's sister, Mag, is staying with us. She can knit cable stitch.' Mum, not interested in sewing and knitting, and, in the shadow of Dad's accomplished sisters, not trying to compete, continued with her practice of her religion and her writing of songs and poetry and letters to the paper about the government. She no longer played her accordion, while Dad's bagpipes and bagpipe music now stayed untouched in the cupboard, and there was no more singing in the evenings. Once Dad took out his oil paints and added to the hunting scene that he had copied from a cigarette card, but he put the painting aside, unfinished, and never painted again, leaving one of the dogs forever without pupils in its eyes. Why? I wondered. It would have been such a small effort to make the two dots that would give the dog sight. Looking back, I think that my father's reluctance or inability to give sight to the dog was an indication both of the extent of his despair and his sense of the imperfection of everything. One could say (as he did again and again) when we children pestered him to finish the picture or to play the bagpipes in the evening, as he used to do, that he 'hadn't the heart any more.'

When Aunty Maggie came to visit us, although she was dying, she brought new life into our home, with news of the outside world, of motion pictures, and new words. The depression was news everywhere. More interesting, however, was the permanent wave. We knew that Mrs Walker, our Wyndham neighbor who had shifted to Gore and kept in touch with us, had written to tell of her permanent wave, causing Mother to gasp in horror at her submission to something so 'unnatural.' And now Aunty Maggie was talking in an ordinary way about people who had permanent waves, and who'd had *second* permanent waves. I knew the meaning of *permanent*. I had supposed that a permanent wave meant just that, and the prospect of a word's lack of truth gave me a feeling of shock. If *permanent* was *everlasting*, like forever, like the stiffly petaled flowers in their bell jars upon the graves, then how could a permanent wave wear out? I was constantly preoccupied with the idea of 'truth' ever since Miss Botting had questioned me on the infant school platform, 'Tell the truth. Why don't you tell the truth?'; although I had learned that the consequences of telling the truth were as dire as those of lying. And now no one seemed to care that 'permanent wave' was not the 'truth.'

Day after day Aunty Maggie sat quietly knitting her cable stitch or sewing her fancy-work, using *Crewel* (which I thought were *Cruel*) needles and Clark's stranded cotton, holding the strands up to the light to count them. She and Mum used to laugh together about the Outram days and the visit of the Duke and Duchess of York. And one evening Mum and Aunty Maggie went to the pictures, the only time Mother ever went to the picures, where they saw *Alf's Button Afloat* and *Viennese Nights*, and I'd never seen such a sparkle in Mum's eyes as she sang (for she still sang as she worked),

As the years roll on
after you are gone,
You will remember Vienna,
you will recall
evenings in May,
sweethearts have gone
and vanished away ...
Where did they come from,
where did they go,
Vienna will never let you know ...

Like all the songs, it was sad, and Mum and Aunty Maggie would look at each other in a homesick way, and Mum would say, 'Oh, Mag! Just think.' And Aunty Maggie would nod her head. And perhaps if Dad were home, he'd say boldly, 'Where's the *Happy Mag*?' The *Happy Mag* was a magazine of jokes that Dad and Mum liked to read, and we, on our first encounter with Aunty Maggie, had thought she was some relation to the woman on the cover of the *Happy Mag*.

And then one day, when I came home from school, I found that Aunty Maggie had gone away; they had taken her to the hospital, where she died. She was buried beside Grandma and Grandad in the family grave, and her husband, Uncle Alex, a stern man who disliked the Frame family, put a bell jar of everlasting flowers on her grave and was reported to have said, 'That's got rid of the Frames!'

Mother, who met every death including the recent one of her father, whom we had never known, with a biblical quote, repeated, 'And God shall wipe away all tears from their eyes; and there shall be no more death, neither sorrow nor crying, for the *former things are passed away*.' The word *permanent*, then, had its own kind of revenge on those who misused it, for the Bible said that nothing was permanent, and everything came and went – the seasons and the animals (Old Cat), the people (Grandma, two Grandads, Aunty Maggie). And Poppy.

Aunty Maggie's visit and death coincided also with the latest expression, '*OK, chief*,' which we children were forbidden to say, but when Dad was at work, we relentlessly pursued our mother, saying, 'OK, chief, OK, chief,' while Myrtle, who as the eldest was very grown up and rebellious, openly defied orders by saying, 'OK, chief' to Dad. *Openly*. The *openly* seemed to be important, for Dad repeated it several times before he sent Myrtle to the bedroom and locked the door. 'You'll get the belt,' he said. They were now at war.

'OK, chief' was best said while you were chewing *chutty* or chewing gum, drawing the chutty out of your mouth and stretching it as you watched the adult alarm at this apparent irresponsibility of speech and appetite. In the continuing arguments between Myrtle and Dad over every new phase of her life – the desire to wear slacks (forbidden), lipstick (forbidden), to go dancing, to go downtown on Friday nights, the chewing gum and the 'OK, chief' were the culmination, those final chewing speaking blasphemies that became, ironically, a remembered part of Aunty Maggie's visit, Aunty Maggie, whom we watched struggling with food and word until she died, with her throat closed up.

Hurrah for the free spit-wheeling chutty and the joyous 'OK, chief'! With a new exuberance, in spite of everything, our life continued.

11

The Prince of Sleep

It was a fact that most of the girls who left school early went to work at the woollen mills 'out the North Road.' We'd see the mill girls riding their bikes in the morning and hear the mill whistle at eight o'clock and at lunchtime and in the afternoon, a sound which shared the otherwise sleepy air of Oamaru, the white stone city, with that of the Oamaru town clock and the constant roaring of the sea on the foreshore. If we climbed the zigzag to the wooden seat of the Beautifying Society and looked out at the view, we'd see in the distance the tall chimneys of the woollen mills. A future spent working there or locked in the industrial school at Caversham which, like the breaking wave, would fall first on Myrtle before it reached me, too, in time, did not deter us from a range of suddenly acquired ambitions.

For all the enormity of our grocery bill and our apparent inability to pay it, Mrs Feather generously decided to give each of us children threepence each week to go to the local pictures on Saturday afternoons, and now that we 'went to the pictures' every week, a new selection of ambitions in a completely new world was offered to us. Myrtle, who did resemble Ginger Rogers with her golden hair, planned to be a dancer or a film star or both, and to start her career, she sent for the free book on Professor Bolot's dancing course, which arrived as a pamphlet with details of the number of guineas to be paid and a large photo of Professor Bolot himself, dark-haired, with a mustache, and dressed in black,, flared Spanish pants, dancing a Spanish dance. I had similar encouragement and setback from my 'free' book on ventriloquism. We gave up sending for instructions, although, some years later, I wrote to Scribe, Amorc, California, for the 'Secrets of the Universe.' Since a blind child violinist had performed at the Opera House, I had dreams of being a blind violinist, but, more practically, because I had curly hair and dimples, I also saw myself as perhaps another Shirley Temple.

Myrtle had some reason for wanting to be an actress, for she played Joan of Arc in the school play, dressed in silver cardboard armor. She played in *The Mikado*, too, and was the captain of the *HMS Pinafore*. She recited over the wireless, too, 4XD in Dunedin, where the sister of the sister-in-law of Aunty Isy was a real wireless aunt, Aunt Molly. We went next door to the Fletts to listen through the static of their wireless to Myrtle's faraway voice reciting her favorite poem, 'The Prince of Sleep.' Or, as we knew it, 'I Met at Eve':

> I met at eve the Prince of Sleep,
> His was a still and lovely face,
> He wandered through a valley steep,
>   Lovely in a lonely place.
>
> His garb was grey of lavender,
> About his brow a poppy-wreath
> Burned like dim coals and everywhere
>   The air was sweeter for his breath.
>
> His twilight feet no sandals wore,
> His eyes shone faint in their own flame,
> Fair moths that gloomed his steps before
>   Seemed letters of his lovely name.
>
> His house is in the mountain ways . . .

There were other verses, too. Myrtle recited them all, showing clearly that she was halfway to becoming a film star. She could run and jump, too, and swim and so would be strong enough to be at MGM or RKO studios sharp at six each morning and yet still be able to go to the Hollywood parties in her backless.

Then, toward the end of the year, when she was running in the school sports, she collapsed and was brought home, and the doctor who came to examine her said she had a heart defect and could die at any time. This was how Mum explained it to us, although she said 'go' instead of 'die,' while we received the news with shocked disbelief, for Myrtle was so strong and alive, with only one scar on her body, where she had tried to walk on stilts in Wyndham, and with her curly golden hair like Ginger Rogers, and her plans all arranged for a film scout to notice her and ask her to sign a contract for millions . . .

For a time we watched and waited, curiously and fearfully, but Myrtle didn't stop breathing, and we soon forgot, for death was stillness, and Myrtle was full of movement and dancing and a wireless star, too, with her favorite poem, 'I Met at Eve the Prince of Sleep.'

With the discovery of Myrtle's 'bad heart,' it was advised that she leave school, and of course she could not work at the mill. Instead, it was arranged that she help Mrs McGimpsey, a widow with two daughters, who lived down the road in a house with a balcony in front. And now that Myrtle had a few shillings each week to spend, she was able to buy lipstick and powder and Friday night milk shakes and the 'forbidden' magazines that we read under the bedclothes – *True Confessions*, *True Romance*, with their photographs of real people, beautiful women and handsome men kissing and cuddling. I had no doubt of the 'truth' of these stories simply because they were labeled 'true stories,' for I had still not learned to accept the deceit of words and had only some weeks earlier rushed into a new shop that had opened downtown, *The Self Help*, expecting to be able to help myself to anything, free!

The 'Truth' was also revealed in the weekly newspaper of that name which Dad bought from Adams's in a bundle known as 'the books.' 'Go down and get the books,' he'd say. And one of us would go down to Adams's and watch fascinated while the one-armed Mr Adams, leaning his stump in its floppy sleeve upon the books arranged on the counter, rolled and tied and snipped the bundle – *Truth*, *The Humour* (the finest collection of the world's wit), *The Happy Mag*, *The Exporter*, for Mum to read the poem or paragraph she'd sent, and our comics.

Although we were forbidden to read the Truth, we did glimpse now and again the blurred photographs of old verandahed houses where the murder had been committed, the unshaven, wild-eyed faces of the criminals or the escaped mental patients, the swampy paddocks with the arrow showing where the body had been found; and although our parents tried to keep from us the news of unsavory events, somehow the facts and rumors of chocolate poisoners and baby farmers managed to reach us. In our parents' view 'natural' disasters, such as earthquakes, tidal waves, even fires, were somehow 'clean' whereas murders, baby farming, shady chemists who did a side trade in abortions, these were too terrible to be discussed or even acknowledged. Even in the realm of the terrible, had our parents known about him, was the old man who sometimes followed us up to the Beautifying Society seat or into the gardens and, smiling in a funny way, opened his fly and showed us his tool. We thought him a joke, giving him the name of *Fizgig* and admitting him to our circle of peculiar people, like old maids and gypsy Ma and the town prostitute and the Catholics and the Germans and Chinese, anyone who was different, with rhymes chanted about them. 'Catholic dogs stink like frogs.' 'Ching-Chong Chinaman born in a jar christened in a teapot ha ha ha,' or the general rhyme that could refer to any race:

> In nineteen hundred and four
> the Germans went to war
> they sat on the rocks
> and played with their cocks
> in nineteen hundred and four.

Sometimes we chanted, 'The Maoris went to War.' We had learned about the Maoris at school, but there were few in Oamaru. Mother had told us how she had been 'brought up among the Maoris' because her mother had step-sisters and brothers who were Maori. And Myrtle's friend was a Maori and yet not a Maori, for her father, Dad's work mate and fishing mate, was described as 'full-blooded,' as if this were something better than his daughter, who was talked of as being 'only a half-caste,' as if it were something to be ashamed of. I gave none of this much thought, only sensing the feeling behind people's words; I thought the word *half-caste* was related to Dad's fishing casts and cast sheep and the worm casts on the front lawn after the rain and the song Mother would suddenly begin to sing because it reminded her of her 'dear old headmaster, Mr Howard':

> Old Tom is cast
> and the Christchurch bells ring one two three four.
> Our Christchurch?
> No, the Christchurch of old Dr John Godfrey . . .

There were so many ways of talking about people, of admiring them or scorning them for the strangest reasons, sometimes just because they were dead or lived in another country; and then people were admired for what they could do, like Aunty Maggie with her cable stitch and the children who danced and sang in the competitions; or for what they had or who their parents were, and even if you didn't know people, you decided about them and arranged your feelings for them and told everyone how you felt . . . in your lofty adult voice; while below, we children caught all the traveling opinions, like falling stars, keeping some and letting some slip through.

At this time in our lives, Mother (who always said of herself, 'I'm firm in my opinions, mind you,' causing us to say as we drank our dock-seed tea or dahlia wine, 'I'm firm in my opinions, mind you, Mrs . . .') had suddenly found herself beset by opinions and advice from all sides. It was Bruddie's illness, you see. While Myrtle and I became best friends and Dots and Chicks became best friends, admitting to their play Molly Robson over the road, Bruddie was ill, day after day and night after night, while Mother looked after him and searched for a 'cure.'

12
Cures

The doctors, Mother said, were little help, prescribing medicine that made Bruddie more confused and angry and stupid, when he was a bright little boy who had walked and talked earlier than the others, except Myrtle. It was Dad's opinion that Bruddie could 'stop his fits if he wanted to,' and for a time, Mother, influenced by Dad's certainty, joined the cry, 'Stop it, Bruddie, stop it at once,' when the familiar signs of an attack began to show. Someone suggested the illness could be 'beaten out of him,' and Dad did whip him once or twice to try to cure him. This failed of course, but Dad maintained that Bruddie could 'stop it if he wanted to.' The anwer, he said, was discipline and will power.

With the prospect of a cure unlikely, Mother began searching for the cause to correct it and once again found herself laden with opinions and advice. 'It could be his spine,' someone said, adding that they knew someone who'd been miraculously cured by a chiropractor who insisted that the answer was always in the spine. So Mother took Bruddie to the chiropractor near the foot of Eden Street, in the large house with the double driveway and the antirrhinums or snapdragons in velvet. The chiropractor was a tall, sallow-faced man in a gray suit. His eyes looked as if he were squeezing something behind them. 'Without a doubt,' he told Mother, 'it's the boy's spine.' For months then, Mother took Bruddie to the chiropractor at ten shillings a visit, although we didn't always pay that, as we had a garden full of vegetables and there was always a catch of salmon or whitebait or crayfish to give away.

For a while, then, the grownups talked to one another about the mysteries of 'the spine,' and the way they talked there was no doubt in my mind that the spine was a great mystery and wonder, in fact, Bruddie's spine was something to be envied. Looking through the doctor's book, the *Ladies' Handbook of Home Treatment*,

69

we children, in secret, stared fearfully at the colored plates showing 'Deformities of the spine,' 'tuberculosis of the spine.' When, however, it became clear that the answer was not 'the spine,' Mother accepted an opinion that said, 'It could be his eyes.' Then followed daylong journeys in the train to Timaru to see the 'eye doctor.' Next – perhaps it was the ears? Once again there were journeys to Timaru to visit the ear specialist.

Finally, it seemed that perhaps the mystery was solved: the answer was diet, a more inexpensive answer than spine, eyes, and ears. Someone gave Mother a book, *Hints on Healthy Living*, where the answer was said to lie in the brown bread and bran – in roughage. 'I knew it,' Mother said. 'Your grandmother with her diabetes was told to drink nothing but cabbage water. Whole wheat and vegetables . . .' Except for not always having brown bread and bran, we had always eaten well, even luxuriously, for there were always big tins of honey and raspberries from Up Central and sacks of oysters from down south and the salmon, whitebait, crayfish, trout that Dad caught.

While Mother's search or pilgrimage continued, we children became more 'wild' and unruly, passionately embracing every craze of town and school and neighborhood; we became members of gangs (The Green Feather) and secret societies. We ripped the backs from the king's dining-room chairs and used them as sledges, first greasing the 'runners' with drippings from the kitchen. We rushed up and down Thames Street, trying to spot the organized mistakes in the shop windows and thus win a prize; we crowded into the newly opened bright-red McKenzies on hearing the news that Frenchies were for sale, only to discover that they were finger-stalls, after all. At home, when the Christadelphians were having their meeting in the dining room or when Mother was talking poetry, as she did with a group of young men who came to the house to read her their poems, we chanted abuse at them, mimicking them, and squashing their hats. The dogs, too (there was Myrtle's Lassie and Bruddie's Laddie and the one or two pups which were always around), joined in our expeditions, rushing here and there, barking their excitement.

It couldn't last. The neighbors, complaining of 'dogs jumping in and out of the Frames' windows,' sent Mr Crump, the health inspector, who arrived without warning and, standing fiercely in the middle of our bedroom, next to the full chamber pot with its mixed shades of amber, and pointing to the unmade bed and the general untidiness, threatened Mother that if we did not get rid of the dogs and if 'those children' didn't do something to help around the house, he would send us to the *Welfare*.

So Lassie and Laddie and the two pups which we had watched having their tails cut off (we were told, but didn't believe it, that it didn't hurt) were put in sacks and drowned in the creek, and about two weeks later Myrtle brought home another black, fluffy kitten, which we kept and which was to become known as Big Puss, mother of generations. Also arrived, perhaps in response to a letter from Mother, was our Grandma Godfrey, whom we'd never met but about whom Mother talked often and lovingly so that, as far as we could judge, Grandma Godfrey was the perfect mother.

13
The Birds of the Air

I disliked Grandma Godfrey at once: she was a stranger, and she behaved toward Mum as if she owned her, when everyone knew that Mum belonged to us, and the saddest fact was that Mum appeared to agree with Grandma Godfrey's ownership, to accept it and enjoy it. How they talked! Grandma saying Lottie this and Lottie that, and Mum calling her *Mother*. Oh, the old times down Waikawa Road, Mr Howard, Mr Stocker, Old Caps, the Piranos, the Kennys, the Godfreys, the Joyces, Heberley, Dieffenbach, the Pebble Path, Wellington and Kirkaldies, on and on into the 'olden days' of the *pioneers* and the *surveyors* with their *white feet* or their *white foot*, like a snail's foot, for Mother always talked of the surveyors as treading with their white foot . . . We knew the stories by heart, and we knew Grandma Godfrey's wonderful nature, of the walks we could have with her 'along the gully,' of her skill in bush craft, her understanding and love. We knew how she would be 'like a sister' to us. 'Like a sister to you, you'll see.' And how the birds of the air, surely with much reason not to trust people, would fly down to feed from Grandma's hand, for all creatures trusted Grandma. We had listened, sometimes interested, sometimes bored, to the stories of Grandma Godfrey, and now that she had arrived, we resented her. She began at once to complain about our behavior, how we 'walked all over' our mother, how we 'cheeked' her, how she waited 'hand and foot' on us when she was not preoccupied with our brother, and how our brother could get better if he 'put his mind to it'; and how our father was a heathen, and 'everything' was the result of Mother's marrying out of the Christadelphian religion; and the house was a pigsty with none of the children 'lifting a finger' to help or having 'any respect.'

We'd heard it all before, combined with the description, 'devils at home, angels abroad.' Mum, her fair-skinned face patched with red, tears in her eyes, her loyalty torn, said nothing. Perhaps she wished that the longed-for visit by Grandma Godfrey had never been. The dreamed-of walk along the gully was a failure. We were self-conscious. We did not respond to Grandma's jokes, for we disliked 'jolly' adults, like old Dr Orbell, cracking jokes we couldn't understand and pretending there was some secret understanding between us. We had our own fun in our own way; besides, we were sick to death of the silly 'pioneers.'

Grandma Godfrey cut short her visit, and her parting remark was that if we were her children, she would take the belt from the wheel of the sewing machine and give us all a sound whipping. Was that *really* Mother's mother? we wondered. Mum's eyes were full of tears again. She knew that we knew now that her own mother had not been so perfect, after all, that she was just like all the mothers around, other mothers that we knew, those that whipped and shouted and wouldn't let anyone walk on their cleaned, polished floors; thin mothers with no lap and no titties; all the other mothers except our own who was soft and went on about nature and God but who would never be cruel to anything or anyone, and when she told us about the birds of the air, flying down to feed from Grandma Godfrey's hand, Mother was really talking about herself, for the little green birds, the wax-eyes, came always and planted their tiny feet in twig shapes in the palm of her hand. And we were sure the birds listened (as we did) when it was raining outside with Oamaru rain, mixed with sea, different from Wyndham rain mixed with river, and Mum looked out the window and sang that sad song,

> Come in, you naughty bird,
> the rain is pouring down,
> what will your mother say
> if you stay there and drown?
> You are a very naughty bird,
> you do not think of me.
> I'm sure I do not care,
> said the sparrow on the tree.

> The little bird was drowned . . .
> So never say you do not care
> for do not care, you see,
> is certain to be drowned
> like the sparrow on the tree . . .

We knew she was singing to the birds and to us, for it was the only way she could warn us that we were not always well behaved . . .

She could not reprimand her family. She was cruel to nothing: well, maybe to the fleas we had when the dogs were alive. Crack crack in the night, and we'd hear Dad saying, 'Got one, got one, you have to crack their backs.' Dad laid the dead fleas in a row on the marble washstand.

Grandma Godfrey did not visit us again. She died a few years later, and the relations sent Mum a small sum of money, about fifteen pounds (which she spent on us) and a dark painting of a storm at sea that was a companion to the other dark painting hanging over the mantelpiece in our bedroom – a mother dead in childbirth surrounded by her mourning family. The *Storm at Sea* hung in the passage, where it was so dark that you could see only the white tops of the waves and the white stone of the lighthouse.

14
Pastimes

Myrtle found a friend to talk to, a Mrs P., widowed or divorced, who lived down the road in a house with an untidy garden where straggly flowers grew through the wire fence. When Myrtle's friendship with Mrs P. became known, the word Dad used was *association*, and the instruction was, 'I forbid you to asociate with Mrs P.' Which meant that her reputation was 'unsavory,' as if it were the promised whirls of vapor arising from a meal cooking. I knew that 'unsavory' could mean many things, from using bad language like 'bugger,' 'OK, chief,' 'God Almighty,' 'bitch,' 'bastard,' or wearing shocking clothes like slacks and dresses with only thin straps over the shoulders or bathing suits with the back cut too deep; or smoking and drinking and going out with boys or loitering downtown on Friday night or outside the pie cart after the pictures. I never discovered why Mrs P. was unsavory, for when Myrtle took me on her forbidden visits to Mrs P.'s place, Mrs P. said hardly a word. She was usually busy rolling pastry (I think she cooked for people) with a cigarette dangling from her mouth. She'd give us something to eat and a cup of milk or tea and listen while Myrtle told her how awful it was at home, with Dad and everything. Sometimes she gave Myrtle a cigarette while I watched admiringly as Myrtle smoked and puffed out and blew smoke rings. I'd smoked pine needle cigarettes in the plannies but never real ones, although I liked to watch Dad with his book of tissues, which he called *tishees*, and his tin of snuffly-smelling tobacco, as he carefully rolled a cigarette, twirling it between his first and second fingers, pulling the loose threads of tobacco from each end, tapping each end, then, starting at the left, lick along the licking-line of the tissue, then closing it, tap it, fatten it a little, then smoke it or stack it in a tin.

Mrs P. taught Myrtle songs that were also thought of as unsavory:

And when I die (and when I die)
don't bury me at all.
Just pickle my bones
in Alco Hall.

I found out later that the word was *alcohol*, known in our family as 'drink,' pronounced differently from ordinary 'drink,' as in 'Would you like a drink of water, of Boston Cream, or lemon syrup?' but with a mixture of fear, horror, and judgment, 'He's fond of *drink*' or 'the drink.'

When our parents heard us singing, 'And when I die . . .' they forbade us to continue.

When I was not going to Mrs P.'s with Myrtle or downtown to look at the boys, I now spent my time with Dots and Chicks, preparing for our lives as actresses and concert performers. Each week the scene was set for the following week by the Saturday afternoon 'picture.' We went to every film, watching through the news, the cartoon, the Pete Smith Novelties, the James Fitzpatrick travel talks, the serial, and, after halftime or interval, the 'big picture.' Sometimes I went with Myrtle, who was keen on Jack Dixon, the projectionist at the Majestic, who lived up the road in a house with a high macrocarpa hedge in front. When the music and the funny pastel advertisements of Oamaru shops had finished and the program was about to begin, we'd see him walk the length of the aisle, go through a small door down by the stage, 'to turn on the sound,' Myrtle would explain, then, returning, walk past us again, along the aisle, to go upstairs to the projection room, and sometimes we'd look up and see his shadow, high up near the ceiling at the back, and Myrtle would nudge me again and say, 'There's Jack Dixon moving around upstairs. The pictures are starting.'

There'd be a funnel of light directed onto the screen, the whirring noise of the film, and Jack Dixon was at work in earnest. He was a neat young man, rather pale but handsome, and the coat of his striped suit was always buttoned in front, the way George Raft buttoned his coat, except that George Raft was a villain.

Each week the manager, Mr Williams, appeared on the stage to announce competitions and to remind the adults about the community sing that was held at the Majestic each week. Mr Williams took the promotion of his films very seriously, and every serial had its special competition. We loved the serials, although our belief in them changed to a cynical tolerance when we realized that the hero and heroine were immortal in spite of those episodes where they lay beneath the stone crusher or in the caves with the sea advancing. Three memorable serials were *The Lost Special*, about a train that disappeared; *The Invisible Man*, who needed only to press a contraption on his belly button to disappear; and *The Ghost City*, a Western. The Ghost City was lettered in our minds, for each week we were given cardboard letters, each a letter of the title, and the person first completing the title won the prize. There was furious searching, swapping, but what could be done with five Y's or three C's? I had a handful of H's. It was no use; we never won.

Then a chance came at the Opera House for someone in Oamaru to make 'the big time' in films. We knew what would happen. We'd seen it often enough in the films and read of it in the *Motion Picture Weekly*: the performance in the small-town theater (Oamaru), the presence in the audience of the Hollywood talent scout, then the contract, Hollywood, and the Big Time, with a house full of white telephones, dresses made of sparkly, scaly stuff like mermaids' dresses when you attended your premiere.

It happened that an Australian company wanted a young actor. Filled with the anticipation of being 'discovered,' we flocked to the Oamaru House to find that when the Australian producer called for volunteers to go on stage and, leaning toward an imaginary mine, cup their hands and cry, 'Look out, there's dynamite down there,' only a handful of children were bold or brave enough to offer. We watched, amused, scornful, envious, admiring, while each performed. Some were scared at the last minute. Some made fools of themselves. Not so Avril Luxon, whose glory shone a little on us, for he lived in the house on the other side of the bull paddock and his father was the butcher, going around with a horse and cart and wearing a striped apron with a worn leather bag like a bald sporran dangling in front, where he kept the money. Avril was a short, stocky boy with a red, freckled face and red hair, but his 'Look out, there's dynamite down there' echoed through the Opera House, and his performance is the only one I remember. He didn't win the part, though. Someone from Auckland, where people were more clever, won the film test and went off to Australia, on the way to Hollywood and the coveted Big Time, while our life in Oamaru settled again to the collection of letters for The Ghost City or playing the film we'd seen that week or writing our secret codes or trying to dance the Highland Fling, the Sword Dance, the Sailors' Hornpipe, the Highland *Chantreuse* (which we knew as the *Shottish*).

Living then changed from its vertical state to one resembling a simultaneous exhibition, with us hurrying here and there to catch up with all the displays; it was as this chapter has been, a selection of views of the Is-Land. There were many more occupations – how can I describe, for instance, the excitement merely of discovering a new shop, a new flower, a song, game, or name; a new fact – 'You can buy pork bones cheap from the bacon factory,' 'You can buy specked fruit from the fruit shop.' Threepence worth the specs. please . . .

Or the visiting of the parts of Oamaru that caused you to shiver with the sense of yesterdays – down by Tyne Street, the grain stores and the tall stone buildings, some untenanted with broken windows (The Ghost City!), down by the Oamaru Mail, near the gas works, which I thought existed only for the destruction of cats and dogs by the authorities and gas itself as something which people used when they wanted to commit suicide. In that part of Oamaru the grass grew up between the stones of the street, and I believed I was in London in the chapter of our history books which began 'when grass grew in London streets,' that it was also the home of the Press Gang, and the place of the Great Fire and the Great Plague, and I'd hear in my mind the cry, written beneath a vivid illustration in our history book, 'Bring out your dead, bring out your dead.'

In our endless games we were reluctant to let Bruddie play with us in case he fell in a fit, and he overcame this exclusion by accumulating power with goods salvaged from the Coquet Street rubbish dump, goods that we needed for our games and plays, and because he owned the furniture when we played house and the theatrical set when we staged plays, he was able to appoint himself as landlord and stage manager (we were happy to have him in the latter role because he was good at organizing and at figures). Sometimes, as landlord, he threatened to turn us out of our house, making use of a situation that was always with us in 'real' life. Each month when the bills came in, Dad ranged through all the fears available to us: one was that we would be turned out onto the street for not being able to pay the rent; yet each month Mother dressed in her best clothes and went to the lawyer's office, Lee-Grave-and-Grave, to pay the rent.

One of Bruddie's welcome finds was dark red velvet curtains that we could use as stage curtains in the summerhouse. Bruddie also provided the 'gold' (a glittering brass chain) for use in *Honest Jacob*, which we adapted from a story found in an old schoolbook, of the man who found gold in the bread and took it back to the baker: an example of honesty. Another was *Hugh Idle and Mr Toil*, similarly adapted, a haunting tale of a small boy who decides to play the wag from school, and everyone he sees in the town is a twin of Mr Toil, the headmaster, in fact, the same man. We found it to be a nightmare tale, as it was for *Hugh Idle*.

Our plays were performed with song items between – 'Morning Has Broken,' 'Deep in the Forest,' 'Now You May Sail, Matangi,' and another that haunted me, 'Tender Wood Dove Softly Cooing in Your Nest':

> In the elm tree gently swaying, take your rest,
> I long to watch your gentle flight,
> your spreading wings' snowy white . . .
> All the day at work I hear you,
> tender dove,
> take my little song to cheer you,
> with my love.

The song haunted me, because as I sang it, I believed and felt that I myself was singing to the wood dove; then, when I sang the line, 'All the day at work I hear you, tender dove / take my little song to cheer you,' I felt that because I did not think of myself as 'working' or being 'at work,' then the song must belong to my mother, whom I thought of as being at work all day and able (unlike Dad, on the train) to listen now and again to the birds singing outside; and so, as I sang, I seemed to be my mother going about my work, feeling lonely and sad and depending on the song of the dove for comfort.

We recited our favorite poems, too – 'Old Meg She Was a Gypsy,' 'I Met at Eve the Prince of Sleep,' and Myrtle sang her special songs, including 'By the Light o' the Peat Fire Flame' and 'The Minstrel Boy to the war has gone / In the ranks of death you'll find him,' singing it as if the Minstrel Boy were a boyfriend of hers, which I half-believed him to be.

Our father, too, had found a pastime to while away his evening.

He'd look at Dots and start to sing the song which, we all knew, terrified her:

> Don't go down in the mine, Dad,
> dreams very often come true.
> Daddy, you know it would break my heart
> if anything happened to you.

That one verse was enough to produce the expected result: Isabel began to cry and crept under the table, and we knew and Dad knew that it was because she loved him so much and couldn't bear to think of his dying in the mine. Dad would then take the gas mask he had brought home from the war and, putting it over his face, advance toward Chicks, to frighten her because everyone knew that was her special fear, and Chicks, seeing the monster and stranger approach, would also hide and cry. The game with me was to stand me in the middle of the room, where everyone could observe my twitches and tics and the funny faces I pulled, and the more I tried to stop, the harder it became. 'Just look at her, look at her, she's got St Vitus Dance,' Dad would mock.

On happier evenings, although Dad did not sing as he used to sing in Wyndham, he sometimes entertained us with his 'hard-boiled egg' dance and song:

> I'd rather have a hard-boiled egg,
> I'd rather have a hard-boiled egg,
> I'd rather have a hard-boiled egg ...

or his 'Ragtime Cowboy Joe' dance and song, which we loved:

> Way out in Arizona where the bad men are
> the only thing to guide you is an evening star ...
> roughest toughest man by far
> is Ragtime Cowboy Joe ...

Ragtime Cowboy Joe. That was Dad. How we roared with laughter to see his performance!

So that was that. I was almost nine years old now. In moments of family despair, when Mother dared to say, 'We should never have left Wyndham,' and Dad agreed, one part of life untouched for me, still perfect, was the world outside, the seasons. The flowers still came out in their proper time, the dandelion seeds or one-o'clocks never failed to float away into the sky, the poplar trees at the corner where the two Miss Darlings lived changed color and lost their leaves, Jack Frost was about (look out, look out!) after our fingers and toes, and always there was the sky and the clouds and my shadow, and in the evening the moon walked with me, and when I stopped, it stopped, too; and I thought of Old Meg:

> Instead of supper she would stare
> full hard against the moon.
> Her brothers were the craggy hills,
> her sisters larchen trees.
> Alone with her great family
> she lived as she did please.

And I thought of 'I Met at Eve the Prince of Sleep,' Myrtle's poem.

15

Gussy and the Invercargill March

I felt desolate at school. I longed for impossible presents, a doll's house, a sleeping doll, birthday parties, pretty dresses, button-up shoes, patent leather, instead of the lace-up leather shoes with their heavy soles and heel and toe plates, hair that fell over my face so I could brush it away, saying, 'My hair's always getting in my eyes . . .' instead of frizzy red hair 'up like a bush' with everyone remarking on it.

I missed Poppy and the cadged flowers, although I'd collected in my mind many good stories since I read Grimm's Fairy Tales, and I especially treasured the story of Pandora and of Persephone and the Pomegranate seeds which were so vivid, bright red, split, with juice oozing from them, that anyone would have wanted to eat them. There were stories of the Australian desert, too, and Central Africa and South Africa, and the stories from the books each was now given as a prize at the end of the year. Isabel's 'The Joyous Travelers,' a kind of Junior *Canterbury Tales*, became a loved part of our play with its *Hop-About Man*. We devised a Hop-About Dance, 'Ring a Ding Dill':

> Ring a ding dill
> The Hop-About Man
> Comes over the hill.
> The Miraculous Pitcher,
> the Little Crippled Boy . . .

Suddenly, in the midst of my discontent and longing, I was promoted to Standard Four, to Gussy (or Reuben) Dimmock's class where I became, inexplicably, the teacher's 'pet.' It had always been other children who were the teacher's pets – pretty little girls with clean hair ribbons – and hair that accepted a hair ribbon as natural – and nice clothes and well-mannered little boys with clean shirts who confidently played their role unperturbed by the certain number of envious and unkind remarks it attracted. You'd always see the 'teacher's pet' catching up to walk to school with the teacher, with a hop and a skip, keeping in step; and in school you'd see the teacher turn habitually to the 'pet,' letting her or him fetch and carry things, smiling at her or giving him the job of special monitor to open the windows with the long, hooked pole or to return the exercise books with the corrected *My Adventure* or *My Holidays* compositions.

How proud I was of myself in Standard Four! Gussy used to sit me on his knee while he taught the class, and sometimes he would give me a small, special table in front of the class to share with his small son, who was known as a 'mongol' and whom I helped with his lessons. And one day Gussy asked us to write a poem beginning, 'When the sun goes down and the night draws nigh . . .'

At home that evening, the writing of that first poem sparked my first argument over writing as an art, for when I read my poem to Myrtle, she insisted that the words 'touch the sky' should be 'tint the sky':

> When the sun goes down and the night draws nigh
> and the evening shadows touch the sky
> when the birds fly homeward to their nest
> then we know it is time to rest.

> When rabbits to their burrows run
> and children have finished their daily fun,
> when the tiny stars come out to peep,
> then we know it is time to sleep.

I disagreed with Myrtle, who then insisted that there were words and phrases you had to use, and when you were writing about evening shadows, you always said 'tint,' just as you said that stars 'shone' or 'twinkled' and waves 'lapped' and the wind 'roared.' In spite of Myrtle's insistence, I preferred 'touch' to 'tint' but in deference to her obvious wisdom and wider knowledge I changed the word to 'tint' when I took my poem to school. But later, when I wrote it in my notebook, I reverted to 'touch the sky,' having my own way.

The poem, the usual kind of child's poem, was a success only in its predictability, for when Gussy sat me on his knee and began reading, the class was able to guess the last line of each verse and so join in with the words. I found that when I 'shared' my new triumph at home that evening, the family was proud of me, and my father promised to bring home a railway notebook from the loco. foreman's office for me to write down more poems. The railway notebooks where Dad, who was union secretary of the Engine Drivers' Union, wrote the members' and the union contributions, had attractive marbled colors on the edges of the pages that set together formed a marbled pattern which fascinated me. Dad's other books were of equal fascination – the bagpipe music books with their peculiar heavy print and signs in code, which we 'played,' reading or conducting from them until, as with almost every household item we touched, we 'wore' them out or, in adult words, 'ruined' them, leaving them torn, written on, with pages missing; the fly book with its leather cover salt smelling and smeared with patches of fish scales, with the parchment pages, the bulk closed by an elastic band, each page filled with brilliantly colored feather flies on hooks with beautiful names like Red-Tipped Governor, Greenwell's Glory . . . and at night Dad would sit at the table and 'read' his fly book, naming each fly as he turned the crackly pages. We were never allowed to touch his fly book, only to look over his shoulder as he 'read' it or to feel the fatness of the closed book. In our ritual of play we sometimes said, 'I think I'll get out m'fly book.' There were homemade books, too, which we laboriously sewed in place and covered with scraps of wallpaper from the wallpaper shop downtown.

The prospect of having a real notebook and being able to write poems, with numbered pages and an index, made us dizzy with delight, for the others would have notebooks too, under the rules of fair play. We were all hungry for words. Seeing a musical film, we were tortured by not knowing the exact words of the songs, and when one day Myrtle brought home a small booklet with the words of the popular songs of the day, our excitement was acute. In what I might call my 'cowboy and prisoner' period, a year or two earlier, I had written in the homemade notebooks the words of the sad cowboy songs – 'The Wheel of the wagon is broken and it ain't gonna turn no more,' 'There's a bridle hanging on the wall, there's a horseshoe in an empty stall . . .' and the 'Prisoner's' song that Poppy taught me, telling it to me as if it were *her* song in the way that Grimm's Fairy Tales were *her* stories:

The pale moon is shining a shining so bright
on the lovers a-wandering by my window tonight.
Their laughter so merry brings tears to my eyes,
as a prisoner I'm lonely for the moonlight and skies . . .

Poppy told me the song one evening when we were playing in the house next door to hers, which was only half-built, with the foundation and the framework exposed to the bright summer moon of Oamaru, and while we played, we were in danger of being cast into prison, for one day the owner had caught us playing there and astonished us (for we thought the house was *ours*) by calling out fiercely, 'Hop it, you. Hop it, you.' We then named him Hoppityou. 'I saw Hoppityou today.'

Under Gussy's care I blossomed then both as a scholar and as an athlete, for Gussy believed that because every child had a special talent he, as a teacher, had to give everyone a chance to discover the talent. Gussy was known as something of a fanatic in the classroom and on the sports field, and being in Gussy's class meant that when you were running in a race you were training to find out if you would qualify for the Olympic team. The slow, awkward children who couldn't read aloud in those excruciating reading lessons discovered they might be future Olympic champions or they might be 'good at' gardening or handwork which, Gussy stressed, were of equal importance, and with such encouragement, some, their confidence returning, even learned to read aloud and recite their arithmetic tables. In spite of Gussy's teaching that all were equal and special, I did have the joy of being his pet, and as I lacked the customary qualifications for such a post, I never discovered the reason for his choice, unless it was that he thought it was the only way to deal with me and my tics and terrors. He inspired everyone. At home we practiced his voice as he, first assistant to the headmaster, marched us into school each morning with his military cry, eeep-ite eeep-ite, eeep-ite while Ernest Calcott beat upon the kettledrum strapped around his neck. We also practiced Gussy's voice at the beginning of a race and the way he had explained each inflexion: 'On your marks.' To be spoken briskly but matter-of-factly. 'Get Ready.' The Get Ready given no more emphasis than usual, in contrast to our suspense-building Gee-e-e-et Re-e-e-ea-a-a-add-dyyyyy. Then the final short, sharp *Go*. We also practiced for that great day, School

Sports Day, when the North School and the South School struggled for possession of the Primary School Sports' Shield, and all the schools marched around the Show Ground Field with the Oamaru Brass Band playing Colonel Bogey and the Invercargill March. 'Now we're in front of the grandstand,' we'd say, feeling again in our stomachs the surge of excitement. 'Now we're coming around the Outside ...' Then ... de-de-de-de-de-dedede ... *The Invercargill March.*

I ran in relays. I hopped, stepped, and jumped. And in the flat race, as soon as the gun went off, I ran as fast as I could, not being able to understand why, if I was running as fast as I could, I didn't come in first instead of my usual third or fourth. I knew I could feel my legs trying their hardest, and I had been taught that if you tried your hardest to do something, you could do it. Everyone was always lecturing us about 'trying,' pointing out the achievements of great men and women and suggesting that they attained their greatness because they tried their hardest, and in our competitive school world, if you tried your hardest to win, you won: everyone said so. I puzzled over this until I realized it was not the 'truth.' I knew truthfully that I ran my fastest in the race. I realized that I didn't win because I didn't have long legs like Audrey Nimmo or extra power like Madge Robertson, the champion dancer, or the other champion dancer from the South School, Beatrice Macfie.

Even Gussy was always telling us to do our best and more or less promising us whatever we wished to have. I was in a mood for homilies that year. Every morning we had longer Scripture lessons taken by one of the local ministers. I always listened intently, but I learned more from the hymns, for as kinds of song they appealed to me. 'There Is a Green Hill Far Away.' 'All Things Bright and Beautiful' (thought of as strictly a junior school song). 'What a friend we have in Jesus. There's a friend for little children above the bright blue sky ...' When I came home singing, 'There's a friend for little children' with its promise of heaven, I found that Mother disapproved because heaven on earth was the Christadelphian belief, not heaven in the sky. Mother explained that when you died, you died, staying in your grave until the Second Coming and the Resurrection and Judgment Day (which I imagined as a heavenly kind of Sports Day with the Oamaru Brass Band playing the Invercargill March and the Pipe Band playing 'The Road to the Isles'). At the Resurrection, Mother said, all would be as they

86

were just before they died and would then be judged as worthy or unworthy, and if they were found unworthy, they would be struck dead again for ever.

'And will everyone wake up on Resurrection Day?'

'Everyone.'

'Even Grandma?'

'Of course.'

'And what about the animals, Old Cat and Lassie and Laddie?'

'The animals have no place in the kingdom.'

Because I could not accept that there was no room for all creatures, I did not adopt Mother's religion. 'There must be room for Old Cat and Laddie and Lassie.' I could not understand why Mother, so liberal in her views of the world and such a lover of 'creatures,' could have them so dismissed from glory.

As that year was ending, I was told that I was Dux of the School, equal with another girl from another Standard Four. Some said it was because I was Gussy's 'pet,' and it may have been so in that he encouraged me in my lessons. On the last day I wore a white dress with a cape collar (sent by Aunty Polly), and as I walked from the stage, having received my gold medal, I suddenly panicked, not feeling the medal where it had been pinned. I hurried back onto the stage, searching the boards until I realized that my medal was still safe. My humiliation was acute when I realized I may have revealed to the world how proud I was to have a Dux medal!

I knew that in being Dux I had pleased my father, and this pleased me, for day by day as I brought home tales of life in Standard Four, Dad had begun to say, 'Well, are you going to be Dux, then?'

When all the excitement was over, I remembered that the envelope presented to me with the Dux medal contained a year's subscription to the Oamaru Public Library, known as the Oamaru Athenaeum and Mechanics' Institute. 'I can go to the Athenaeum free,' I said, not quite sure what *Athenaeum* meant. And in the holidays, when one day I went to the loco. foreman's office with a hot pie for Dad's lunch, I heard Dad say, 'My daughter goes to the Athenaeum.'

16

The Athenaeum

The Athenaeum was a two-storied building in Thames Street with the lower floor used as a museum for caged rocks, pieces of bone, greenstone, and stuffed native birds, including a huia labeled extinct, while, guarded at the foot of the stairs by a huge glass-eyed reconstructed moa also labeled extinct, the upper floor contained the library where the librarian, named, I supposed, from her own habitat, Miss Ironside, sat behind an iron grille, issuing and returning books. The Juvenile Section (Fourteen and under Twenty-One Silence Please Do Not Turn the Leaves Down) consisted of one wall of books by the windows overlooking Thames Street.

'Books' meant books mostly of the English language for reading, as opposed to those other books I knew – the bagpipe music, Dad's fly book; Dad's union books; God's Book – the big Christa-delphian book with pictures of God in a swirl of cloud and thunder; the Bible; the Doctor's Book, with instructions on childhood sickness and a chapter on the lying-in woman who, the illustration showed, was 'bearing down' pulling hold of a sheet attached like a roller towel to the iron bed head; the autograph books with their pastel-colored leaves; the birthday books (Mother's, the Whittier Birthday book); our numerous homemade books; the comic books; our school books; and lastly Aunty Maggie's 'needle books' with flannel pages pierced in formation by Crewel (Cruel) needles.

'What will I get from the library, Mum?' I asked, suddenly ignorant and feeling in awe of the world of books in a library, having no idea what to choose and clinging to Grimm's Fairy Tales and the School Journals, and the poems I knew, and having no desire to read the 'children's' books I was meant to have read – *Alice in Wonderland*, *The Wind in the Willows*, *Peter Pan*, the *Just So* stories ... Mother, in a rapture, exclaimed, 'Oh, Mark Twain (Samuel Clemens), *Innocents Abroad*, oh, *Uncle Tom's Cabin*, oh,

David Copperfield (Dickens, oh, the *Christmas Books*, kiddies, it's a cold night, said the King of the Goblins).'

My new library subscription was a family affair. I brought home for Bruddie a 'William' book, which we all read. I found Grimm's Fairy Tales, the same kind of red-covered book with the thin pages packed with black print that I'd borrowed from Poppy. I found a Western for Dad and a Dickens for Mum, who had no time to read it but who touched it and opened it and flipped the pages and read out striking descriptions, saying, 'How wonderful, kiddies, Charles Dickens, born in poverty, growing up to be a great writer.' Then, after a prolonged season with the Brothers Grimm, I became bold enough to read other books – The Bumper Books for Girls and Boys, Boarding School books, while I continued, on the side, as it were, with Myrtle's *True Confessions* and *True Romances*.

Summer holidays again. Endless play, make-believe, roaming the plannies, the hill, the gully. My days at the Oamaru North School over, I looked forward to the junior high school, learning French and algebra and geometry and singing and hearing new poems. The junior high school also held the junior and senior high property room, full of scenery and stage clothes and masks, all described to me by Myrtle; and there were the teachers, they, too, made famous by Myrtle's descriptions of them. And in particular there was the French family of the French book that I'd already tried to read – Marcel and Denise and their parents Monsieur and Madame Desgranges.

Going to junior high school meant, however, wearing a special uniform that, unlike the uniform at the Oamaru North School, was compulsory and included the correctly pleated light gray flannel tunic, winter and summer hats (black beret or black felt and white panama, with regulation hatbands), blouses, summer and winter, white cotton and gray flannel, black stockings, black pants, black shoes, with gym shoes for sports. Fortunately, the Dux medal, which gave me the library subscription, had also reminded relations who might have forgotten that the Frame girls might need clothing if they were 'going on' to high school; and so there arrived a parcel of assorted clothes from Aunty Polly and from Aunty Isy – 'aunt-smelling' clothes in 'aunts' colors,' brown, purple, maroon, dark blue, which we divided amongst ourselves but which did not help toward a school uniform. Mother gravely faced the man in Hodges to buy 'on tick' some gray flannel from which she tried to make a tunic, which turned out as a disastrously sewn and shaped hybrid garment, neither tunic nor dress, with a curiously cutaway yoke that exposed most of the front of my bunched white blouse (bunched because I was growing, and a larger size saved money in advance). Although I knew that my school tunic was 'funny,' it did not worry me at that stage of my life, for I was too much engrossed in the prospect of new lessons, of Marcel and Denise, and 'Bright is the ring of words/When the right man rings them,' another of Myrtle's poems learned at junior high.

17

Clothed in White Samite

Our teacher in the first year was Miss Romans, known to everyone as Iris Beatrice who, in the language of the time, was rumored to be 'fast,' a sherry drinker, a bridge player, a party-goer – known qualifications for 'fastness.' Also, she was pretty, and she wore high heels.

Of that junior year I remember little apart from the fastness of Miss Romans (which I never observed in action) and the fact that she wore a black gown and moved her elbows as if she were flying, as she walked into the room; and I remember the delight of learning French words and songs and the names of science apparatus (Bunsen burner, litmus paper); the cooking lessons, lemon sago, puff pastry, cream crackers; how to scrub a wooden table; the sewing, embroidery with the eternal *Crewel* needles and the Clarks stranded cotton, all of which had to be bought and therefore asked for at home and the reply endured, 'You'd be better off working at the mill,' and the final consent received under the weight of that Dux medal and the new parental dream, 'She's going to be a teacher like Cousin Peg, who emigrated to Canada.'

There might have been a time when the supply of crewel needles and stranded cotton, the pens, pencils, nibs, blotters, compasses, set squares, protractors, rulers, exercise books 'ruled feint with margin' (at which Dad made his joke, 'Faint all right, at the cost of all this'), journal covers, journal pins . . . all might have ceased had not that year, 1935, become the year of the first Labor government with its promise of Social Security, free medical treatment, free hospital treatment for all. Our debts to the doctor and the hospitals were then so enormous that we had given up hope of paying them, and Dad, with his skill as a fisherman, was still making peace offerings of salmon, trout, whitebait, and crayfish. The election of the Labor government was almost like a Second Coming, so great was the joy in our household, and so revered the new prime minister, 'Micky' Savage, whose poster-size photograph was now pinned to our kitchen wall, where it stayed for the rest of the time we lived at Fifty-six Eden Street, and even when the Second World War was declared, Micky Savage was moved only slightly to make way for the map of the world with the tiny pinned flags, 'Flag the Movements of the Allied Forces from Day to Day.'

When the Social Security Act was finally passed, Dad, in a spontaneous dance of delight in which the family joined, removed the bills from behind the clock and, taking the poker from its hook by the stove, lifted the cover and thrust all the bills into the fire. Mother, a true Godfrey (all the Godfreys were known as 'weepers'), wept, and we children made whooping cowboy shouts of joy. And from that day, as each political hero and heroine appeared on the scene, Micky Savage, John A. Lee (especially revered because he was a writer), Bob Semple, Mabel Howard, Paddy Webb, took pride of place beside Longfellow, Dickens, Mark Twain, John Greenleaf Whittier, Cousin Peg, the Godfrey, Joyce, Frazer, and Nash ancestors. And when, a few years later, we bought a wireless on tick and Parliament was broadcast, Mother went about her everlasting work with the wireless switched to Parliament while she made her own interjections, and as each speaker finished, she praised the 'goodies' and criticized the 'baddies,' using the first names of the members and talking of them and to them with an intimacy that not even our old friends and neighbors, the Walkers, John and Bessie, forever known as Mr and Mrs, could claim, although, unlike the MPs, the Walkers came to us for holidays and sent their daughter to our place for her honeymoon.

It was in my second year at Waitaki Junior High School that, making up my mind to be a 'poet' when I 'grew up,' I began to write poems regularly in my small railway notebook. This renewed interest was prompted no doubt by our teacher's interest in poetry: devoted to verse speaking, she gave us a number of haunting poems to learn and recite, and although I objected to the singsong way she expected us to speak, some of that singing trapped me, with my passion for songs, in a world that seemed to have no boundaries and was part of the world of Old Meg, the beggars and swaggers, angels, too, and Poppy and Hoppityou and the Twelve Dancing Princesses, and the playground songs, and like to the tide moaning in grief by the shore, E pare ra. Also, Miss Lindsay used to read for hours from Tennyson's *Idylls of the King*, as if it were her personal poem, and it was partly her absorption in it that compelled me to listen and wonder. I can still see her as she gazed toward the classroom door, as if toward a lake, saying 'an arm rose up ... clothed in white samite, mystic, wonderful ...' as if she had experienced it, as if the jeweled sword Excalibur 'all the haft twinkled with diamond sparks/Myriads of topaz-lights, and jacinth-work/Of subtlest jewellery ...' had been a part of her life that she, like Sir Bedevere, was reluctant to give up. She mourned, too, the passing of Arthur, in a way quite unsuited to *our* Miss Lindsay with her ordinary brown clothes and patchy face:

> And call'd him by his name, complaining loud,
> And dropping bitter tears against a brow
> Striped with dark blood ...

Miss Lindsay conjured up with equal vividness the Last Minstrel, 'The way was long, the wind was cold/The Minstrel was infirm and old ...' all in a world of cities and kingdoms new to me, a part of history not found in our history books, for whereas our history books encouraged unalterable opinions of characters, certain kings and leaders being irrevocably 'good' or 'bad' or 'weak' or 'strong,' with their actions permanently described thus, in the world of King Arthur and the Last Minstrel and the Duke of Wellington ('Who is he that cometh like an honoured guest?'), we could think or feel as we wished toward the characters, or as the poet, discounting history, invited us to; we were the poet's guest, his world was his own kingdom, reached, as one of the poems told us, through the *Ring of Words*:

> Bright is the ring of words
>   When the right man rings them,
> Fair the fall of songs
>   When the singer sings them.

This other land revealed to me by Miss Lindsay, whom we laughed at because her face was like a cow's face, with a dewlap, and she wore funny shoes with pointy toes, could contain all the unspoken feeling that moved alive beneath the surface of each day and night and came above the surface only in the way earthworms came, when there was too much rain; and these feelings were secrets that this new land could receive without shock or horror or the need for revenge or punishment; it was yet a private place, even described by Miss Lindsay when she read the lines:

> A place
> where no one comes
> or hath come since the
> making of the world.

I brought home news of the poems, reciting them again and again, with Mother receiving them as an exile receives sight of a long-lost native land. 'We had "Ring out Wild Bells" today,' I said, whereupon Mum, with a gasp of recognition, repeated, 'Ring out wild bells to the wild sky/The flying cloud, the frosty light . . .' to be joined by Myrtle, a most recent exile, saying in a homesick voice, '"The year is dying, let him die . . ." We had that.' It was enough to remind Myrtle of 'The Minstrel Boy' and 'I Met at Eve the Prince of Sleep' and Un-deux-trois-quatre-cinq . . . , the knowing of which gave her a power and satisfaction that she hadn't found in her new life of growing up and arguing with Dad and going to dances and seeing Jack Dixon operate the projector at the Majestic. 'We had *The Lay of the Last Minstrel*, too,' I told the family, whereupon Mum exclaimed, 'Oh, Oh. Sir Walter Scott. *The Lay of the Last Minstrel*.'

Her favorite poems were those of first and last, the newly discovered and the long lost, all of which seemed to fuse with her preoccupation with the 'latter days' creating opposite images of total darkness and loss with total light and revelation. This feeling, in its simplest form, prompted her pity for all that had been left behind or abandoned or neglected. In contradiction to her denial of the 'Kingdom' to animals, she wrote verses about stray cats and wounded birds and also about deserted gardens and houses and days that had been, and in her choice of subjects she influenced me. I wrote about 'days gone by':

> The pine trees whisper as they sway
> caressed by some kind gentle breeze,
> sadly, lonely through the day
> bringing back sweet memories

concluding after two more verses with,

> A memory, half-forgotten day
> so full of spring sunshines
> told by trees that gently sway
> and whispered by the pines.

I wrote poems about everything around me. I wrote a poem about the sand, the sky, the leaves, a rainbow (taking care to list the exact colors – 'orange, yellow, red, and heliotrope, a lovely green and blue.' I wrote about Marie Antoinette and the Palace of Fontainebleau:

> Ah, Queen of Sorrows, I wish you were here
> to see the sunset, a beautiful pink,
> you might take a book and sit by the mere,
> or stoop to the crystal and drink.
>
> The times are hard, the smiles are few
> there is bloodshed and many men die,
> no time to look at the rainwashed blue
> or the sunset in the sky . . .

I wrote, too, about a mystery ship, 'I gazed at it through seablue eyes, my old old mystery ship . . .'

Inevitably there was the poem about my mother, whose reverence of motherhood inspired her to write many such poems and who kept reminding us about other 'strays' of the world, 'Don't forget, she may be somebody's mother.'

I enjoyed writing my railway book. I kept an index of poems, and I remember part of the first index:

> Captain Scott.
> Sand.
> A longing.
> My Rainbow . . .

My poems were a mixture of conventional ideas about 'poetic' vocabulary and the cowboy and prison songs recorded in my other notebooks and the contents of the small popular song books brought home by Myrtle and the songs sung by my parents and grandparents. I continued writing my poems, sensing the approval of my parents – of Mother, who saw the birth of something she had mourned as lost from her life, whose overwhelming might-have-been was *publication* of a book. She once sent a collection of her poems to Stockwells, England, which advertised regularly in New Zealand newspapers and magazines, and her joy at having the poems accepted for publication was lessened only by the knowledge that she couldn't afford the sum of money they quoted for publication, and although she resigned herself to never having the money, she could say proudly now and again, 'I've had a book of poems accepted for publication by Stockwells, Ilfracombe, England.' Nor could she afford to copyright a song that won first prize in an Australasian competition, for when she sent to the copyright office for the necessary document ('I've put in for the copyright of my song'), she found there was a fee that she could not pay, and so the song remained uncopyrighted. She was left with knowledge of the procedure, however, and she often talked of it: 'I have an application for copyright of my song.' And over the years her recollection became more fruitful than disappointing, 'I've been in touch with the copyright office about my song.'

Mother talked of 'Fleet Street London' also, making it part of her dreams, and it could have been that her tolerance of our reading of comics was the result of our discovery in the small print at the end of the comic 'Printed at Farringdon House, Fleet Street, London EC4.' Her response to this discovery was rapturous, 'Oh, kiddies, Farringdon House, Fleet Street, London EC4.'

We ourselves in our modest way communicated with Fleet Street, London, in unanswered letters requesting free badges, booklets, trinkets. Mother talked of publication and of Fleet Street, London, with the same longing as that with which she talked of Bruddie's recovery ('When you grow out of it, Bruddie . . .'), for the magic instrument was now thought to be natural growth, and of the Latter Days and the Second Coming and the Resurrection, and, on a more domestic level, of the icing set with which she would some day write (the ultimate domestic literacy) words and phrases on the Christmas and New Year cakes she baked each year. Words and phrases that could be eaten!

Dad, remembering Cousin Peg and my Duxhood, also showed delight, of a more restrained kind, in my writing of poems. Described by Mother, rather sadly, as 'like all the Frames, a dour Scot, your father's a dour Scot, kiddies,' Dad was yet a glutton for jokes, listening eagerly to the comedy on our newly acquired wireless, and reading the jokes in the *Happy Mag* and *Humour* before he cut the paper into squares as wiping paper for the lavatory; yet he seemed to be unable to accept that funny events happened in real life, in his own home, and he listened glumly to Mother's laughter as she recounted the many humorous events that she still found in each day, both at home and over the wireless.

Dad's interest in words was formal. Words were to be sought and explained and not used for 'airy-fairy' purposes, and although he was proud that I was writing poetry, his special interest was in letting others know and in hoping it might win prizes. He liked to sit in the evenings, working out puzzles in magazines and organizing words in crossword puzzles. I, who disliked most puzzles, particularly jigsaws after the experience of being left always with a spare piece of sea or sky or grass beside an already completed sea, sky, and lawn, used to feel a shock of pride when Dad asked me to help him with the crossword. I felt as if the King of the World were enlisting my help, but I'd conceal my feelings and work very calmly to find the word. I remember one evening, hour after hour, with one word to be found, and Dad refusing to give in, and I, infected with his determination, searching and searching, and although bedtime came, neither of us gave in and early next morning I heard a shout of triumph from the kitchen, where Dad was getting ready for work.

'*Rattan*. It's *rattan*.' And it was *rattan*, a word that was new to me but that remains memorable in my life with *decide, destination, adventure, permanent wave, OK, skirting board, wainscot*, and others.

The fact that I was allowed to continue my library subscription (it was now unthinkable that the family should not have access to so many books) also strengthened the interest in writing. There were other influences, too. The year was 1936. There had been an epidemic of polio (known then as infantile paralysis) with cases of meningitis, and there were still isolated cases, with the number expected to increase over the next summer; and attention was focused on the 'crippled children' who had overcome their disability – notably, Gloria Rawlinson, the child poet. It was the time, too, of the Hollywood 'child stars': Shirley Temple, Jane Withers, Freddie Bartholomew. The surge of performing children, of their ambitions and the ambitions of the parents, was at its height in Oamaru and elsewhere, and particularly in our home there was a continued association between disability and proven ability, as Mother repeatedly tried to console Bruddie with stories of Beethoven and his deafness, Milton and his blindness, Julius Caesar and his epilepsy, with the implication that surely Robert Frame of 56 Eden Street, Oamaru, had a life to look forward to in the hope of either a miraculous recovery (for God performed miracles daily) or the development of a talent that could bring him fame and fortune, or, fame and fortune being of this world only, that would allow him to wander in the Garden of Beatitudes, living meekly, poor in spirit, a peacemaker, a mourner for all that was lost and missed, and, in the end, inherit the earth as a child of God.

Whatever the reasons, the children of the town and the province and the country began not only to perform and dream of performing their dances, songs, piano music, violin music, drama, but also to write their own poems and stories, encouraged locally by the children's pages in the newspapers – in Otago by Dot's Page for Dot's Little Folk, of the *Otago Daily Times*. Dutifully we children wrote our letter in its conventional form, 'Dear Dot, Please may I join your happy band of Little Folk. I am so many years old, etc., ending with 'Love to all the Little Folk and your own Dear Self.'

In spite of the embarrassment of the effusiveness of 'your own dear self,' I wrote my letter, asking to be known as 'Golden Butterfly,' an unoriginal name that, already taken, Dot changed to *Amber Butterfly*. The others, except Chicks, who was given the name she asked for, Dancing Fairy, also had their chosen names changed – Bruddie's Sergeant Dan (after the Royal Mountie on the Creamota packet) became Sergeant Dick, Myrtle's Good Queen Bess was changed to Good Queen Charlotte, and Isabel's Apple Blossom to Apple Petal.

Continuing the emphasis on the disabled, sometimes a blind pianist or violinist or a 'crippled' singer performed over the wireless, with the announcer, aware, too, of the number of children being 'struck down' with infantile paralysis, stressing the performer's disability as if it were somehow a part of the ability, even necessary to it. I came to link the two. I perceived that in a world where it was admirable to be brave and noble, it was more brave and noble to be writing poems if you were crippled or blind than if you had no disability. I longed to be struck with paralysis so that I might lie in bed all day or sit in a wheelchair, writing stories and poems. That is, if I could not, as I also longed to do, learn music and dancing and singing, performing at the regular competitions, winning prizes that would enable me to go to Hollywood.

The year ended. I received two small leather-bound books for a prize and a bursary for five pounds to help me 'go on' to senior high school, where there were three courses – professional or academic, commercial, or domestic, with no mixture of subjects as in the junior high school. My parents, now taking it for granted that I would become a teacher, decided to allow me to continue at school, although Dad warned me that if times were hard, I might have to leave school or change to 'commercial' and work in an office. Most of the girls in our neighborhood planned to leave school in their third or fourth year to work in shops or offices, and most were to take a commercial course. Poppy, whom I saw distantly now and again, exchanging formal greetings, was to take 'commercial.' I had already suffered the corruption of literature by taking to heart yet another of my favorite poems – 'Old Grey Squirrel,' by Alfred Noyes, where a young boy dreams of a life at sea, and when he grows up, his dream unfulfilled, he works in an office, slowly 'dying inside.'

> He is perched upon a high stool in London.
> The Golden Gate is very far away.
> They caught him, and they caged him, like a squirrel.
> He is totting up accounts, and going grey.

In my mind that high stool could be found in Oamaru, in the lawyer's office where Mother paid the rent. A gray tired-looking man perched there on a high stool before a high, sloping desk, working at his accounts, and when he came to take the rent money, I could see his nose sharp like a pen-nib with a drop of nosey instead of ink on the end. Such was my trust in the 'truth' of literature that I believed the Alfred Noyes version of commercial life, looking on life in an office as a betrayal of anyone's dearest dreams. 'I'll never take commercial,' I said vehemently.

Acres of Christmas holidays lay before us. There was the celebration of Christmas which, with New Year's Eve and Guy Fawkes Day, were happy family times. On Christmas morning there were always presents in the stockings (Dad's gray work socks) lying on the macrocarpa branches in the dining-room fireplace, seldom the presents we asked for but welcome and exciting because they were presents and surprises; and on New Year's Eve, after the Scottish tradition, there was first-footing and a midnight feast with the laden table that promised plenty throughout the year. Then, on Guy Fawkes Night, year after year, we stood in the backyard while Dad lit the sparklers, Catherine Wheels, and the one skyrocket, while we lit our penny crackers and threw our throwdowns.

At Christmas there was always the beach, Oamaru's Friendly Bay to go to, or sometimes an excursion to Timaru's Caroline Bay. And the Christmas holidays of this year had already been spent in swimming, for Miss Lindsay had unceremoniously taught me to swim by pushing me in the baths, as I had refused to submit to her usual method of teaching, which was to tie a belt around the learner's waist and haul her along by a pole attached to the belt. However great the shock of being pushed in, I was now a keen swimmer.

So we spent the days at the beach or the baths. Myrtle and Isabel were both good swimmers. Myrtle was also a good diver, and at the town baths we'd watch our favorite divers on the high or low springboards, and then Myrtle would have her turn at diving her special dives. We had discovered that the baths were a better place to watch the boys, because they were either in the water, easily observed, or stretched out on their towels at their end of the baths by the diving boards, or flexing their muscles and showing off because they knew they were being watched. When Jack Dixon started going to the baths, and we saw how pale his skin was, not at all like Errol Flynn's or Clark Gable's, Myrtle lost interest in him. 'He's weedy,' she said. Weediness was a boy's ultimate disgrace.

So, from our vantage point on the seats, we watched the boys arriving and leaving with their towels and trunks draped around their necks, and we heard their casual reference to their 'togs,' whereas we arrived with our 'togs' carefully rolled in a parcel under our arm and left with them again rolled tightly, and as we went out into the street, we endured with a certain delight the way the boys flipped their towels at us in a gesture of challenge while we, our togs rolled more tightly than ever, walked haughtily on our way home.

Then, as the days moved from quiet blue January into February and another summer, they were long and hot and full of cloudy doom and weariness. I dreaded returning to school, for I needed yet another school uniform for the senior high, another tunic, dark gray serge, with a black felt hat and black beret for winter and a white panama hat for summer; gray flannel blouses and white cotton blouses as for the junior high, a white dress for the garden party at the end of the year and the school breakup in the Opera House; and a colored girdle, the color depending on which of the

100

four Houses, named after the first four principals of Waitaki, we were balloted into. Fortunately, Aunty Polly had volunteered to sew my school tunic and, hoping that all would be well but dreading that it wouldn't, I waited for the parcel from Petone.

Everything that had been summer blooming was in the first stages of decay; the fluffy asters in every pastel shade were curling and browning at the ends of their petals; the cream banksia roses of the summerhouse were already shriveled and fallen. We lay on the parched front lawn, looking up at the clouds, interpreting their shapes, asking, What do you see? What do you see?

18
Picnics

We found a friend that summer – Marguerite, who with her parents and her elder sister Noraleen and her young brother John had lately shifted to the house across the road. Marguerite overwhelmed us with her difference, her different mannerisms, speech, vocabulary, clothes, her parents, her house, even her religion, Roman Catholic, which meant that she attended a different school and was taught by nuns. A born actress, she took advantage of her *glamor*, insisting, truthfully or not, that she was really Spanish. Her beguiling certainty about everything left no room for us to doubt her. As soon as we met her, we began to replace what we now thought of as our tired unsuitable vocabulary with Marguerite's more interesting words – a writing table became an escritoire, a sofa a chesterfield, a costume an *ensemble*. Her mother had clothes, too, in contrast to our mother's wet sugar-bag aprons and torn singlet-dresses for ordinary days and the navy blue costume for paying the rent or taking Bruddie to find a cure – that costume having been bought mail order, to fit, from Glasson's Warehouse, Christchurch, and paid for at so much a week. This first venture into time payment wasn't made lightly; it was like a loss of financial virginity. With visits to the doctor and Bruddie's hospital treatment (for times when the fits would not stop) now free, we were able to buy blankets, too, on time payment and a quilt, also bedsheets for visitors. Mother subdued her uneasiness in using time payment for 'material goods' as opposed to the ordinary grocers' and butchers' bills, with the remark that we were valued customers, which indeed we must have been, for every six months a cyclostyled leaflet arrived from the firm, in the form of a letter which began, 'Dear Valued Customer . . .' And we did indeed pay our bills. We had almost paid Mrs Feather's long-standing bill.

We were relieved to find that Marguerite's mother and father also had bills. Her father had more than one suit, and in his work he didn't get covered with oil and coal on his blueys, nor did he carry a leather workbag with his lunch (salmon sandwiches or onion sandwiches), bringing home lumps of railway coal to feed the kitchen fire and railway notebooks to feed our craze for writing.

During the Easter of 1936, as a celebration of the election of a Labor government and the possible arrival of the days described in Uncle Scrim's song,

> There's a new day in view,
> there is gold in the blue
> there is hope in the hearts of men . . .

we went for our first family holiday, on the train to Rakaia, traveling in a first-class 'bird cage' on our annual free ticket. Dad had arranged everything. A lorry carrying bales of straw met us at the station and brought us (all on the back of the lorry) along country roads and through paddocks until we came to the river bank where we pitched our bell tent. Dad put straw in one corner for our beds while Mum arranged the food, including the tin of water biscuits, near the entrance, and we fetched wood for the fire, and after the billy had been boiled, and Dad had warned us that if we touched the inside of the tent while it was raining, it would leak, Dad set out with his salmon-fishing gear – his rod and reel and new shining spoons and fishing bag – to find a salmon pool. My recollection is that we children spent all weekend exploring the gum trees, listening to the magpies, watching the hawks, avoiding the inevitable Jersey bull, eating the water biscuits, while Mum kept the fire going and made cups of tea, sitting with a wet hanky over her brow, her face glistening in the sun, her fat legs in their wide shoes stretched out, showing their sores, big red patches, blotched with Rexona ointment, green, medical-smelling, which she smeared on the sores in the hope they would vanish. She sat there reciting poetry, making up humorous rhymes about Dad and the salmon he would catch and the ones that would get away and about the time Dad and Jimmy Peneamene caught a salmon that vanished,

> One day when Jim and I went up
> to the house for a bite and sup,
> someone stole into the shed

where we were to lay our head.
Someone stole our salmon,
someone stole our salmon . . .

Or she sat staring beyond the willows to the raging green (snow-fed, kiddies) Rakaia and talked of her 'girlhood' and its perfection.

Then, during the night, when the rain up-country made the river rise to within a few feet of our tent and we were forced to get up in the dark and move the tent to higher ground, we felt we had experienced the adventure of our lives, the kind of adventure that other children with their many holidays seemed to take for granted.

Now, having our new friend, Marguerite, we had a chance to tell again the story of our adventure, reliving the water rising, the escape, the magpies, the water biscuits (a whole tin of water biscuits!), the salmon eaten round the camp fire, crossing the bull paddock to Langley's farm for milk, all the grizzles, the laughs, and the nights lying on our bed of straw, playing games of pretend, listening to the river sound, daring each other to touch the canvas to see if what Dad had said was true and finding that it was, fighting and making up, planning, dreaming, comparing our past, our glories, our bodies; then, outside again, gathering manuka for the fire, trying to make flutes out of willow, trying to divine water, staring dreamily at the river and the swirling branches and the occasional dead sheep or cow flowing down to the sea. With Marguerite as our audience, our 'Last year we went camping to Rakaia' became 'Every year we go camping to Rakaia.'

And when Dad decided that we would go again to Rakaia these holidays and we asked Marguerite to come with us, she accepted, and once again we began our Rakaia stories, overjoyed that 'someone else,' someone who lived in the usual kind of house with the usual kind of parents and family, with ordinary happenings that were not disasters or nightmares, would share the Rakaia glories. We began at once to behave like couriers, treating Marguerite as if she were about to become a tourist in a foreign land. There was some doubt at first about traveling, as the epidemic of infantile paralysis had worsened and the newspapers each day reported the mounting number of cases. There was talk of the schools being kept closed until the peak of the epidemic was over. On the other hand, Mother believed that in a tent under God's open sky, away from the crowded cities, we were out of reach of the epidemic.

Also, she had faith in our health. Had she not breast-fed each of us until we were big enough to start biting her? Did we not have enough milk in our early years, with always plenty of fish to give us brains, tins of honey, vegetables from the garden, and fruit, and coarse oatmeal to keep our bowels open?

Once again at Rakaia we explored, played, ate, boasting to Marguerite, yet submitting to her foreign power, speaking her language, playing her games. Myrtle wore her gray slacks, which everyone, even Dad, accepted now, for many women had begun to wear slacks. Women smoked, too. Marguerite's mother smoked and wore makeup, this adding to Marguerite's glamor. And how we envied her mysterious life with priests and nuns and Confession and holy water.

At the end of our memorable sunburn-filled holiday Dad took our photographs with the box camera he'd bought at the auction in Wyndham, which he used when relations came and we had our photos taken at the gardens, standing on the Japanese bridge. When the photographs of Rakaia were developed, Mother gave a gasp of horror when she saw that in one of the photographs Myrtle appeared to be transparent: all except Myrtle had taken flesh and blood photographs. It made her feel afraid, Mother said, everything coming at once, the death of Grandma Godfrey, the beautiful Rakaia river, snow-fed, flashing green and blue, the southern Alps with their autumn snow, the epidemic that filled the country with sadness and dread, and the sight of the victims who'd escaped severe paralysis, walking about with their leg irons to support them; all combined to bring to the surface the buried fear that Myrtle might die at any time.

19

A Death

The school year began. The schools were not to reopen. We were to have lessons by correspondence. My school tunic arrived from Aunty Polly. It fitted closely, with two instead of three pleats, but I was satisfied enough to let Dad take my photo to send to Aunty Polly.

As if school holidays and summer had been destined to go hand in hand, yet another summer came, with hot winds, nor'westers burning from the Canterbury Plains, copper sulphate or 'blue-stone' skies, and no place for comfort except the water, the sea, or the baths, with us going back and forth from both. And on the last Friday before the book lists and the first school lessons were to arrive, Myrtle suggested we go swimming first and then go downtown to look at the boys, but I refused, interested now in my lessons, how to get my new books without too much pleading and argument, wondering whether I'd like senior high, thinking, too, of the notebooks I would fill with poetry. Myrtle and I quarreled about my refusal to go with her; only the quarrel was really about me as 'Dad's pet' because I'd been Dux, and I was now going to senior high, to be a teacher like Dad's Cousin Peg, who immigrated to Canada; I was entering the world that Myrtle had once shared with Joan of Arc and the Prince of Sleep, with the promise of many more wonderful characters lost; besides, Dad was cruellest to Myrtle, who was rebellious, daring, openly disobedient, always under the threat of being sent to the industrial school at Caversham, whereas I who wanted only to be 'good' and approved of, was timidly obedient except where I could deceive with a certainty of not being caught.

As a result of that afternoon quarrel, Myrtle went with Marguerite and Isabel to the baths while I stayed home, dutifully preparing myself for the new school year. It was late afternoon when someone knocked at the door, and Mother, thinking it was a salesman, opened the door, said quickly, 'Nothing today, thank you,' and was about to shut the door in the man's face when he, like the stereotype of a salesman, wedged his foot in and forced his way into the kitchen, while Mother, who had told us tales of such actions, prepared herself to, in her usual phrase, 'floor him.' I was standing by the door into the dining room. The man glanced at me and said sharply, 'Send that child away.' I stayed and listened. 'I'm a doctor,' the man said. 'I've come to tell you about your daughter Myrtle. She's been drowned. They've taken her body to the morgue.'

I stared, able only to absorb the news, 'They've taken her body to the morgue.' We children had always fancied we knew which building was the morgue, a small, moss-covered stone hut down by the Post Office, near where the Oamaru creek rolled green and slimy over an artificial waterfall. We used to frighten one another by referring to the morgue as we passed it on our shortcut through Takaro Park toward Tyne Street and the beach, and sometimes we tried to look through the small barred window ('for air, so the bodies don't smell') to see within. The place was so small, sealed, inaccessible that we knew it must be the morgue, and when we spoke of it at home, Mother had always shown fear, which encouraged us, after the many examples from our teasing father, to repeat the word.

'Morgue, morgue.'

'Don't say that word, kiddies.'

Now, when the doctor had delivered his news and gone, Mum herself spoke the word, for it had convinced her, too, that Myrtle had really died. 'They've taken her to the morgue,' she said.

This sudden intrusion of the word *morgue* into our lives, where before it had been a forbidden word, with us now saying it openly, made me feel grown-up, accomplished, and alone. Myrtle was dead, drowned. At first I was glad, thinking there'd be no more quarrels, crying, thrashings, with Dad trying to control her and angry with her and us listening frightened, pitying, and crying, too. Then the sad fact came home to me that there might be a prospect of peace, but the cost was the entire removal of Myrtle, not just for a holiday or next door or downtown or anywhere in the world, but off the face of the earth and out of the world, a complete disappearance and not even a trial, just to see how it worked. And where would be the fun-loving, optimistic, confiding, teasing

107

Myrtle with the scar on her knee and the high instep ('it proves I'm cut out to be a dancer') and her grown-up monthlies, and the ambition to go to Hollywood to be a film star, to tap-dance with Fred Astaire, singing and dancing her way to fame and fortune? Where would be the Joan of Arc with her painted silver armor and helmet, the wireless performer who recited 'over the air':

> I met at eve the Prince of Sleep,
> His was a still and lovely face.

Myrtle's entire removal was stressed when she didn't come home that night to do the things she ordinarily did, to finish what she had begun in the morning, bring in the shoes cleaned with white cleaner and left to dry on the washhouse window sill in the sun. Dad came home early and put his arms around Mum and cried, and we'd never seen him cry before. And everyone seemed to forget about Isabel, and it was quite late, almost dark, when Isabel came in, her fair hair still wet and bedraggled from swimming in the baths, her small, scared face telling everyone where she had been and what she had seen.

That night we cuddled in bed together, and as the next day passed and the next, with the grown-ups talking about inquests and coroners and undertakers and Mother naming each with a sharpness of tone that allowed them to take a share of the 'blame' and the talk of the funeral and the mechanics of burial, I gradually acquired a new knowledge that hadn't reached me through the other deaths in the family; but this was Myrtle, her death by drowning, her funeral notice, her funeral, her flowers, her coffin, her grave; she had never had so many possessions all at once.

After the inquest, when they brought her home in her coffin into the Sturmer-smelling front room and Mum asked, 'Do you want to see Myrtle?' I said no. 'We'll see her on Resurrection Day,' Mum said, conjuring once again in my mind the turmoil of Resurrection Day, the crowds, the wild scanning of faces, the panic as centuries of people confront each other and only a miracle provides room for all.

Myrtle was buried, her grave covered with wreaths from many people in Oamaru, including the Swimming Club where she had been a member, and some of the boys that we'd watched showing off with their muscles and their togs. And soon the rain rained on the flowers, and the ink on the cards was smudged, and the colored ribbons frayed and rotted, and the grave itself sank until it was level with the earth. 'It always sinks, you know,' they said.

And one afternoon, when I was putting fresh flowers on Myrtle's grave and crumbling aspros into the water in the jam jar because 'they' had said aspros made the flowers last, I saw Miss Lindsay nearby visiting her mother's grave, Miss Lindsay of the 'jeweled sword Excalibur and the arm clothed in white samite, mystic, wonderful.'

'Is Myrtle there?' Miss Lindsay asked.

I nodded.

'What are you putting in the water?'

'Aspros,' I said. Miss Lindsay's suddenly gentle tone and her ooze of understanding infuriated me.

'They won't bring her back,' she said gently.

'I know,' I said coldly, explaining the reason for the aspros.

I had lately learned many techniques of making flowers and other things 'last,' for there had suddenly been much discussion at home and amongst people who came to the house to offer their sympathy in our 'sad loss.' They were obsessed with means of preventing the decay of their 'floral tributes,' of preserving the cards and ribbons. They spoke of Myrtle, too, of keeping her memory 'green.'

'And you'll have photos of her, too, Lottie,' they said to Mother (as they sat patting and arranging their 'permanent' waves). And that was so, for when we finally realized that Myrtle had really collapsed in the water and been drowned, that she was never coming home again to wear her clothes and sleep in the bed and just be there, everyone searched for recent photos and found only the 'ghost' photo taken at Rakaia and one other, with us all in our bathing suits, I with a beginning titty showing where my shoulder strap had slipped; but it was Myrtle's photo that was needed. The photographer downtown was able to extract Myrtle entirely from that family group, although he was forced to leave behind one of Myrtle's arms that had been around Marguerite. Undaunted, the photographer fashioned for Myrtle a new photographic arm and at last presented us with a complete, enlarged photo of Myrtle. Everyone said how lucky we were to have a recent photo, and only those who knew could discern the grafted arm.

20

Once Paumanok

The epidemic continued. The school sent its list of required texts and exercise books and a questionnaire about our choice of subjects. I found I could 'take' either Latin or geography, but the decision was made for me by Dad, who compared the prices of the two textbooks. 'You'll take geography,' he said.

Somehow, allowing for the goodwill of the two stationers, W. E. Adams and Jeffrey and Smith, I was able to buy on credit all the books I needed as well as an expensive item like a geometrical set. My excitement was tremendous – the new books, their color, their smell, the algebra and geometry and arithmetic books all with *answers* at the back. To be trusted with answers to all the problems! From the secretive way the teachers always dealt with and revealed answers, I had concluded, naïvely, that we were taught mathematical calculations at school to collect answers, like prizes, at the end, like a quiz show; I realized now knowing how to arrive at the answer, even if the answer were wrong, was more important; also knowing how to state the question or problem. My heart swelled with a feeling of adulthood at the thought that I'd not have to ask the teacher for the correct answer to each problem. There were books of French fairy tales, too, the first of the series: *Contes et Legendes,* which touched me with its extraordinary rightness and timeliness, with the stories from Grimm's Tales and others revealed in another language, presenting a richness that I felt to be like receiving a fortune. There were the Shakespeare Plays for study, *A Midsummer Night's Dream* with a companion volume, *Approach to Shakespeare,* a book of ancient history, and a book of poems, *Mount Helicon.*

I completed my first set of lessons, writing the inevitable My Adventure composition. I began to explore the poetry book, and to my amazement I discovered that many of the poets knew about Myrtle's death and how strange it was without her. After the funeral was over, the visitors had gone and my new lessons arrived, the everydayness of life had returned; yet in each day there was a blankness, a Myrtle-missing part, and it was upon this blankness that the poets in Mount Helicon were writing the story of my feelings. I could scarcely believe their depth of understanding. Mother, who revered all poets, was right, as usual, and her habit of murmuring from time to time 'Only the poets know, only the poets know' was now explicable to me; I understood also why she wrote so many of her verses about poets: there was the one I had recited at school,

> He was a poet, he loved the wild thunder
> as it crashed in the Universe. Now he sleeps under,
> under the grass he loved. Stilled now his hand
> only a poet's heart could understand.

> He heard whispering of the pine trees.
> Always within his heart, sweet melodies.
> Glories of morning awoke in his heart.
> He was himself of nature apart.
> Softly he slumbers. Does someone care?
> Nature showers o'er him leaves from her hair.

Mother sought the poets not necessarily for their poems but for the romantic idea of them, as if they might be a more tangible Second Coming, and when she began her familiar praise of them, Dad became jealous, as he became jealous of her references to Christ, and his jealousy always resulted in scorn.

A long poem in *Mount Helicon, The Lost Mate* from *Sea Drift* by Walt Whitman, told everything I was feeling – the two mocking birds, the disappearance of one, the long search by its mate, with all the false alarms and pondered might-have-beens, the anger and regret and the desperate reasoning that enlisted the help of magic, ending in the failure to find what was lost and the letting go of all hope of finding it. I understood all the deceptions of thought and feeling which tried to persuade the mourning bird that there'd been no loss, that its mate would soon be home, had simply 'gone away' for the day or had been delayed and would be home some time, 'you'll see.' I read the poem to my youngest sister, Chicks or June, who also understood it. She and I read the poem again and again. I was amazed that my book should contain other such poems about Myrtle – 'Annabel Lee' – 'It was many and many a

111

year ago/In a kingdom by the sea ...' A kingdom by the sea! Oamaru, without a doubt. Oamaru with its wild sea beyond the breakwater and the friendly bay safe within, with the sound of the sea in our ears day and night.

There was yet another poem, 'Evelyn Hope':

> Beautiful Evelyn Hope is dead!
> Sit and watch by her side an hour.
> That is her book-shelf, this her bed;
> She plucked that piece of geranium-flower,
> Beginning to die too, in the glass ...
>
> Sixteen years old when she died!

What marvelous knowledge of the poets who could see through my own life, who could be appearing to write poems of people in Oamaru, which everyone knew was halfway between the equator and the South Pole, forty-five degrees south, and which yet was not nearly so well known as Auckland or Wellington or Sydney or London or Paris, any cities in the Northern Hemisphere where many of the poets (who were dead) had lived! Another poem, beginning, 'The pines were dark on Ramoth Hill,' told how,

> my playmate left her home
> and took with her the laughing spring
> the music and the bloom ...

Ramoth Hill? Surely that was the poet's way of writing of the Hill, our hill, and the pine plantations, the plannies?

> And still the pines of Ramoth Wood
> are moaning like the sea,
> the moaning of the sea of change ...

I understood that the poets, of course, invented many details, changing names and so on, as Poppy and I had called Hoppityou by *our* name for him and not by his real name; I knew that the poets had *woods* where we had *bush* and their pine woods were our plannies. They were also inclined to exaggerate goodness and beauty, for Myrtle was not really beautiful nor was she 'my darling'; she had just been my teasing, pinching, thumping elder sister who knew more than I and who would some day have had music, boys,

112

clothes, love, a mansion – all the fruits of the Hollywood Big Time.

The epidemic over, the schools reopened, and I set out to Waitaki Girls Senior High, wearing my new uniform but discarding for home use only the blazer that Aunty Polly had sewn the wrong color. The schools were so particular about our having the correct uniform, and anything that made one's appearance different from the others was a cause for alarm and worry. We had to be in step always, just as in the early days of Miss Lindsay when she marched us into school with her intoned orders, 'Toes meet the floor first, toes meet the floor first . . .,' when any girl's faltering or misplacement of foot brought her a sharp rebuke.

Our third-form class was small, with eighteen girls, and as we brought a reputation for verse speaking and for being a 'bright' class, the headmistress, Jessie Banks Wilson (known as J. B.), engaged a special elocution teacher to continue our verse speaking. Miss H. was young, pretty, with black hair and rosy cheeks; she was 'soft' and a target for mischief. The poems she taught us were, I felt, less distinguished than the elocutionary exercises accompanying them – 'Three tired toads trying to trot to Tilbury Towers . . . Round the rugged rocks the ragged rascal ran . . . Peter piper picked a peck . . .'

> Mumble and Mutter are muddlesome men
> making mistakes again and again.
> Three grey geese in the greenfield grazing,
> Grey were the geese and green was the grazing . . .

So we chanted our way through our 'set' pieces – The Pipes of Pan, Tarantella, The River (Clear and Cool), none as haunting as Miss Lindsay's 'arm clothed in white samite, mystic, wonderful,' 'Bright is the ring of words when the right man rings them . . . I Met at Eve the Prince of Sleep . . .' Myrtle's poem.

The year was memorable for the French Fairy Tales, for the poetry, for new music, and the study of ancient history, tales of people, cities, animals, birds, insects, that were now vanished 'from the face of the earth.' Once again I called to mind Mother's teaching of creatures extinct and civilizations buried beneath land and sea, and how when we brought home the fossilized shells from the caves on the hill, she had reminded us that Oamaru had once been beneath the sea. This change in civilizations and land and sea forms pointed for her toward the 'latter days' and the time when not only the past would be changed. I sat in the ancient history class, dreaming my dreams of the Sumerians, how they lived, what they wore, the Phoenicians, the Tyrian traders, half-listening as Miss Hall, our form and history teacher, a fair, transparent person with a custard kind of personality and hair that was pale brown with the light showing through it, taught us from our book of ancient history.

I found solace in such learning of all those new worlds, of changes in the past; I felt able to observe more clearly the present changes in our home since Myrtle's death, the new fearfulness shown by my father, not in keeping with his usual forcefulness and dominance of the household. Although he did complain when we girls asked for clothes that we could not have, as our school tunics had to be worn in and out of school, he was no longer angry with our demands, even with our 'Other girls wear ordinary clothes at home,' which he ignored or countered with 'Do you have to do everything the other girls do?' Instead, he began to concentrate his anger and disappointment upon our brother, who had somehow missed the mellowing, for Dad still believed that in some way Bruddie's epilepsy was Bruddie's 'fault,' that he could stop it if he had more control over himself. Dad now turned to him, mocking and scorning him, criticizing his every move while Mother, on Bruddie's 'side,' tried to explain, and the explanation failing, reverted to biblical quotes, 'Blessed are the peacemakers for they shall be called the children of God.' 'Although I speak with the tongues of men and of angels and have not *charity* . . .'

Another world new to me was that of the kind of music I had not known before, introduced to me by the songs in our Dominion Song Books and by one of the girls in the class. Her name was Shirley Grave, and I first became aware of her through the teachers' complaints about her lack of order, her absentmindedness, which were apparently balanced by her imagination. 'Shirley has imagination. She writes poetry.' 'What a dreamer you are, Shirley! Always lost in your poetic world of imagination!'

I looked with interest and envy at this girl who had the poetic attributes I longed for. I wanted to be a poet, and I knew that poets must be imaginative, dream great dreams. No one had ever called me imaginative or poetic, for I was a practical person, even writing poems which were practical, with most never failing to mention some new fact I had learned or giving lists of people, places, colors. For example, my poem about Scott's Expedition read,

> Oats Evans Bowers Wilson and Scott
> by the world forgotten not . . .

For all my ambition, no one could have called me a poet!

Also, I was clever at mathematics and enjoyed working out problems, whereas the 'Shirley has imagination . . . What a dreamer' comment was usually made when Shirley became confused over a mathematical problem.

Then, at the Music Festival, Shirley sang 'To Music,' from our Dominion Song Book.

> Thou holy art in many hours of sadness
> when life's hard toil my spirit hath oppressed . . .

I felt that I had never heard such a beautiful song, both in the piano accompaniment and the words. I learned at the festival that Shirley also played the piano, that only three girls in the class did not study the piano. And then, to make perfect Shirley's enviable endowment, her father died, and while Shirley was absent, the teacher told us about the death and reminded us to be kind to Shirley because her father had died.

I was overcome with envy and longing. Shirley had everything a poet needed plus the tragedy of a dead father. How could I ever be a poet when I was practical, never absentminded, I liked mathematics, and my parents were alive? Well, I thought, if I can't be the necessary dreamer, I can at least pretend, and so I wrote a poem about dreams, believing that if I used the word *dream* repeatedly, in some way I would be creating dreams.

> I dream of misty hills at dawn
> I dream of skies when it is morn . . .

How could anyone, reading those lines, deny I was a dreamer?

I sent my poem to Skipper of 3YA who unexpectedly gave it a prize in a poetry competition. My poem was read over the wireless, and because I was genuinely surprised that it was judged to be good, I supposed that the word *dream* had had its effect; therefore

115

in future poems I used the word *dream*, particularly as I now noticed that most of the poets were using it, perhaps engineering the same deception. 'Tread softly lest you tread on my dreams . . . We are the musicmakers, we are the dreamers of dreams . . . They have their dreams and do not think of us . . .'

I began to collect other words labeled 'poetic' – *stars, gray, soft, deep, shadowy, little, flowers* . . . some having begun as my words in my poem but being used, in the end, because they were the words of 'poetry,' and because poetry emphasized what was romantic (dim, ineffable, little, old, gray) I felt that I was well on the way to becoming and being known as 'poetic and imaginative,' although I was wretchedly conscious that I had none of the disability esteemed in poets: I had not even a parent dead. There had been Myrtle's death, of course, and in the poetry lessons her name was often mentioned, 'Yet once more ye laurels and once more ye Myrtles . . .' written of a drowning too . . . and hearing the name in class sent such a piercing shock through me that I clenched my toes and gripped my hands on the lid of my desk to stop myself from bursting into tears. Somehow, Myrtle's death did not really 'qualify'; it was too much within me and a part of me, and I could not look at it and say *dreamily, poetically,* 'Ah, there's a tragedy. All poets have had tragic lives.'

My brother's illness did not 'qualify' either; it was too present. No one seemed to be able to accept it as possible. Mother still talked of 'when you grow out of it, Bruddie.' There was no schooling for him. He educated himself with books that I brought home from the library and from the many books, originally from the library but now marked *Canceled*, that he found in the town rubbish dump and brought home on his trolley. There was little hope of a job for him, for when he did find one, someone would disclose that he had epilepsy, and he'd be dismissed. 'They found out about me, Mum,' he'd say bitterly.

My father concentrated his attention more and more on the 'abilities' of his daughters. Each day, when I came home from school, he'd say, slightly in jest, mostly in earnest, 'Were you top of the class today? Who did you beat today?' He learned the names of our 'rivals' at school and would ask, 'Well, did you beat M. or S. or T. today?'

This attitude was not unusual; it prevailed in the classroom among the 'top' girls who were forever comparing notes and answers and marks. The competitive spirit flourished throughout the school, and if you were near the 'top' as I, to my surprise, found myself, you lived in glory and privilege, whereas if you were among the 'rest,' you suffered constant sarcasm from the teachers. A selection of four or five girls, who were not, however, among the top scholars, maintained a concentration of power and privilege through sheer personality and so were less likely to suffer the taunts directed at the slower pupils. This group was the core of the class with their activities at home and at school the source of most of the class interest and news; the rest of us moved on the outside in more or less distant concentric circles, looking toward the group whose power, in effect, surpassed even the glory of the scholars who, after all, were sometimes known contemptuously as 'swots.'

On the rim of the farthest circle from the group which was my usual place, I found myself with a tall, asthmatic girl, Shirley's friend, who talked constantly of her brothers at university, quoting them incessantly, with their quotes being chiefly from Karl Marx. Karl Marx says this; Karl Marx says that . . . I sat with this girl for lunch while she explained communism and talked of Karl Marx while I looked with envy toward the place where the group sat, eagerly talking, shaking with laughter as they recounted what *Mummy* and *Daddy* had said and done during the weekend at the *crib* by the sea. The power and happiness flowing from them were almost visible as they talked. Their lives overshadowed the lives of the rest of the class; even Karl Marx was no match for them. Their families were happier, funnier, more exciting, than any others; and they all lived on the fabled *South Hill*. Even the teachers could not resist them, giving them regularly parts in class play-reading while we others watched and listened enviously. It was they who traveled on the Golden Road to Samarkand, who lived through *A Midsummer Night's Dream* and the *Merchant of Venice*; Portia, Titania, Puck, were among them while the rest of us had to be content with playing lone fairies or first, second, or third voices offstage.

At the end of the year I was given a prize, *Boys and Girls Who Became Famous*, which I and my sisters and brother read eagerly during the holidays. We came to know and love the story of the Brontës – the bleak setting of the Yorkshire Moors, the parsonage, the churchyard. We felt close to the self-contained family with the 'wild' brother, the far-off parents going about their daily tasks, the Brontës with their Moors, we with our hill and gully and pine plantations. They knew death in their family, as we had, and their lives were so much more tragic than our life which, in spite of everything, was predominantly joyful, that we could give them, thankfully, the sad feelings which sometimes overcame us, and giving our feelings to the Brontës was a much more satisfying exercise than offering them to Jeanette MacDonald and Nelson Eddy, the current 'stars' with their fulsome musical pleas of

> Sweetheart sweetheart sweetheart
> will you love me ever . . .

Even my cherished cowboy songs and sad poems ('The dog at his master's grave') could not receive what we gave to the Brontës and what I now gave to the newly discovered music ('Thou holy art in many hours of sadness').

I felt that I was no longer the mourning bird of 'Once Paumanok.' I felt that life was very serious now. I thought sometimes, with curiosity and apprehension, about the state known as the future.

21

The Hungry Generations

Some time during that year I had a brief meeting with Poppy, now also at senior high school, taking her commercial course. The word *commercial* aroused so much horror in me that I could scarcely believe in Poppy's survival. If I walked beneath the windows of the classroom where the 'commercial girls' did their work, I could hear the sound of their typewriters and imagine the doom waiting for them.

I met Poppy near the corner of Glen Street by the bank of ice plant where years ago we had squeezed the juice out of the ridged stalks to magic away the warts on our hands. The forbidding of our friendship, the absolute, even proud, acceptance of our parents' ruling, and our completely separate lives since then, gave us a special, distant interest in each other's life now, and when Poppy repeated in a matter-of-fact way, 'You know I'm taking commercial,' I felt a snobbish sense of betrayal, for *everyone* knew that *commercial* girls were a little beneath *professional* girls, and I did not want Poppy to be despised.

'Yes, I'm doing shorthand, typing, double-entry bookkeeping.'

How could she!

'Do you like commercial?' I asked politely.

'So many grammalogues,' Poppy said.

I did not know of grammalogues.

'We're learning grammalogues all the time.'

'Oh. Are you?'

There was a resigned air, a seriousness about our meeting. We could have been two soldiers on a battlefield, exchanging notes about our possibility of survival. The seriousness was somehow accentuated by our dark gray serge tunics, the mark of *Seniors*. The woven girdle around Poppy's tunic was red, the color for Burn House; mine was green, for Gibson. We stared at each other, noting these facts.

Then, suddenly, Poppy seemed to come to life, the same old Poppy who defiantly insisted that other people's flowers growing through the fence belonged to us, we had a right to 'cadge' them, the Poppy who showed me geraniums, their stain and smell, the Grimm's Fairy Tales Poppy.

'We're having "Ode to a Nightingale,"' she said. 'It's in our *Mount Helicon*.'

I'd not read 'Ode to a Nightingale,' my dislike having been aroused by a poet who could go into such boring detail about his feelings as to say, 'My heart aches, and a drowsy numbness pains/ My sense . . .'

'We have to learn some verses,' Poppy said, beginning to recite:

> Thou wast not born for death, Immortal Bird!
>   No hungry generations tread thee down;
> The voice I hear this passing night was heard
>   In ancient days by Emperor and clown:
> Perhaps the self-same song that found a path
>   Through the sad heart of Ruth, when, sick for home,
>   She stood in tears amid the alien corn;
>   The same that oft-times hath
>   Charmed magic casements, opening on the foam
>   Of perilous seas in faery lands forlorn.

Poppy's recitation took me by surprise. She spoke with passionate intimacy as if the poem were directly related to her, as if it were a milestone in her own life. She'd given me so much all those years ago, and now, at Glen Street corner, near the bank of ice plant, she seemed to be making, reluctantly, her declaration of withdrawal from childhood, even in the way she appeared to accept Keats's description of all our lovely fairylands as 'forlorn.' The inner noise and desperation of 'No hungry generations tread thee down' haunted me, though I scarcely understood it; the words swept out of Poppy like a cry of panic. Why? The poem seemed to be so unrelated to her, the 'commercial girl' with the shorthand-typing and double-entry bookkeeping; yet she had proclaimed the poem and its contents to be her very own.

Her recitation had the reality of a precious parting gift that I did not know how to take because I could not understand it. In my ignorance, not even familiar with the biblical story of Ruth, I thought only of a girl at school, Ruth, who had left school early to have a baby; and having no experience of nightingales, my Eden Street having been filled night and morning with the moaning and cooing of the pigeons of Glen Street, and with the chattering of the flocks of goldfinches that haunted our garden, I felt the reality only of those 'hungry generations,' the perilous seas, and the faery lands forlorn.

'We're learning it by heart,' Poppy said again, breaking the spell.

'We haven't had it yet,' I said, talking, as we did, of literary works as if they were a disease.

'I must go,' Poppy said.

We said good-bye. I never talked to her again. I heard that she left school at the end of that year and soon married and settled in one of the coastal towns of Otago.

22

The Kingdom by the Sea

The summer holidays convinced me that Myrtle had really vanished forever. Almost every Sunday during the year we had visited her grave, which was now just another grave among graves with dandelion, dock, chickweed, beginning to grow there. We stopped going to the cemetery. Myrtle was gone. The days of *Secret Confessions*, *True Story*, *True Romance*, the violent quarrels, had rushed by, and I, now the eldest girl who was going to be a schoolteacher like Cousin Peg, who emigrated from Scotland to Canada, did my best to smooth the surface of life, to be, in a sense, invisible, to conceal all in myself that might attract disapproval or anger. I had no close girl friends at school and no boyfriends. I looked on Marguerite as I looked on Poppy – from a distance as part of the past and another life, and high school with its prospect of years of study, homework, examinations, gave me a new, serious life without play. I still belonged to the Athenaeum and Mechanics Institute, having read through all the books in the juvenile library but not yet eligible to begin on the adult section. Reminding the family that I would soon be in the fourth form with more study and homework, I was allowed to shift into the front room, where before only the dead and guests had slept, with the Sturmer apples in the corner, far enough from the kitchen to stifle my ears to the arguments beginning to center now on my brother, who was about fifteen and had discovered the billiard room downtown, the equivalent in those days of a fun parlor, looked on as a den of vice.

We girls usually spent the evening doing homework, writing or listening to the wireless – Dad and Dave of Snake Gully, Fred and Maggie Everybody, The Japanese Houseboy, the Quiz shows, Parliament in session, and the hour-long Inspector Scott of Scotland Yard with its ritual ending, 'All right, take him away,' and titles such as 'The Case of the Hooting Owl,' 'The Case of the Nabob of Blackmere.' We were also enthusiastic listeners to the children's sessions – Big Brother Bill of 4YA with his nature session and Skipper of 3YA with the serial, 'David and Dawn in Fairyland,' introduced by a music which we always wished would last and which we thought of as 'David and Dawn' but which I learned a few years later was 'The Dance of the Flowers' from *The Nutcracker Suite*. We still had dreams of performing – singing, dancing, playing some musical instrument; we still haunted the local competitions, gaining admission to a cheap afternoon session and desperately trying to memorize the steps of the dances so that we might practice them at home. We wrote regularly also to *Dot's Little Folk*, with Monday morning full of excitement for me as I cycled down on Dad's bike to buy the meat and the paper (sixpence worth the skirt steak, twopence worth mince and the paper), and when I'd bought the paper, I'd sneak a glance inside the back page to see our letters or poems and Dot's remarks.

The school year began once again, and once again I had a small bursary of five pounds, which helped in the buying of books. There were the usual worries about money and an increasing worry for me about my school tunic, which was now too tight over my growing breasts but which had to last me until I left school. And there was a feeling of being nowhere, not being able to talk about life at home, and seeing the apparent confidence and happiness of the other girls in the class, particularly those in the Group, all of whom returned to school. One or two had left school, including Shirley, whose widowed mother, it was said, could not afford another year for her. When I heard that Shirley ('To Music Thou holy art in many hours of sadness/When life's hard toil my spirit hath oppressed . . .') was working at the Polytechnic or Bulleids or some place like that selling 'notions' – ribbons, laces, cotton (Clarks Stranded), Crewel Needles, I felt a dreariness and a sense of waste: Poppy taking 'commercial,' Shirley working in a shop, like a repetition of 'Old Grey Squirrel':

> They caught him, and they caged him, like a squirrel.
> He is totting up accounts, and going grey.

What about the 'hungry generations'? And the practice of the 'holy art in many hours of sadness . . .'?

I realized that I *was* a dreamer simply because everywhere reality appeared to be so sordid and wasteful, exposing dreams year by year to relentless decay.

Once again my memory of the year, with Miss Gibson as our form teacher, is of the delights of French and English literature and the excitement and formality of the mathematical problems and the geometry theorems: Given to Prove. Construction. Proof. Conclusion. We were again a small class, with another larger professional fourth form separated from us by the double doors that were opened for English lessons and occasional mathematics and French. The room was the old assembly hall with the honors board and the lists of war dead. The large 4B class, most of whom, unlike us, with our years at junior high, came directly from country schools or – a crime in Miss Gibson's eyes – were 'bus' girls or boarders, became the target of Miss Gibson's or Gibby's sarcasm, while we, 4A, sat smugly nurturing our feelings of superiority.

Our class still contained the Group, now rulers of the Fourth, able to impose upon the rest of the class their taste in dress, manners, leisure activities, films, books, and their opinions on all topics. I used to observe them closely, fascinated by their power. All were neatly dressed with correct complete school uniform, even those items that were optional and that few of the others could afford. There was P., chubby, freckled, a natural comic who held the attention of all at lunchtime when she recounted those adventures at the weekend crib with Mummy and Daddy. Her father was an auctioneer. There was M., small, dark, an accomplished pianist (her mother was a music teacher), a writer of nobly patriotic essays, a generous, thoughtful girl invariably voted the most popular in the class. Her father also was a auctioneer and from time to time mayor of Oamaru. Then there was B. (her father, too, an auctioneer), an accomplished dancer who won many prizes at local and national competitions, a champion runner, too, and 'good-looking' in the accepted style of the time. The artist of the group was L., a pretty, dark-haired girl, whose father was a carpenter and who always won the art prize. The last member was J., another comic, thin, known affectionately as 'Skinny,' awkward, intelligent, with a sharp imagination that was not always appreciated and of which the teachers were often unaware. She was, in the accepted sense, ugly.

Apart from the Group, but at times moving within it in a kind of fourth-form dance, were J. and M., who was also an accomplished pianist with depth and stillness in her playing. She was small, and like most of the others, 'pretty.' Somewhere, at some time, I had been infected with a snobbishness that caused me to wonder why L., whose father was 'only a carpenter,' became part of the Group. The occupation of one's father did matter, in the class and in the school, and it was possible to survive and flourish on an accumulation of the resulting prestige of having an illustrious father (mayor, councillor, doctor, dentist) or a relation who was such or (as in the case of one of the girls) having a double helping – W.'s father was manager of the woollen mills and her cousin was a teacher at Waitaki!

I remained part of the small group of 'scholars' who compared their answers to problems and often worked ahead of the others on extra mathematics. The brightest of our group was usually W. (her father, the manager of the woollen mills), who lived beside the school and had a large doll's house on her front lawn. W. was advanced in reading, too, having read all the children's classics – *Alice in Wonderland*, Kipling's *Jungle Books*, *Toad of Toad Hall*, and she knew the answers to questions that we thought obscure and unanswerable, such as quotes from poems we had not read or heard of. She was the girl to whom my father referred when he said to me, 'Well, did you beat W. today?'

I longed to be close to my father. Sometimes he still asked me, 'How did the sheep look at you?' and dutifully, after all those years, I'd hide my face and put on my 'sheep look' as a way of sharing painlessly with my father. I shared the crosswords, too, and the quiz sessions and the detective stories that he had begun to bring home – small square books, in appearance like the 'love' and the 'boarding school' and the 'Westerns' that we girls read now and again. These were the *Sexton Blake Library*. I despised the way they were written; yet I kept my criticism to myself, dutifully reading each new volume.

'I read the latest Sexton Blake,' I'd say to Dad. 'It's pretty good.'

Dad would answer (the gratitude in his eyes made me pity him), 'Well, it was so-so. I'll bring home some more in the weekend.' I felt, now, that I could see through my father's feelings, and the tragedy I thought I perceived filled me with sadness. When Mum happened to say, 'Both Jean and her father like reading those detective books,' I felt an inordinate pride and gratitude.

And while I read 'Sexton Blakes' at home and study books and other books from the library, the Group was reading Rafael

Sabatini, Nordhoff and Hall (*Mutiny on the Bounty* books), Georgette Heyer (*These Old Shades*), all of which I refused to read because my choice of reading was my area of rebellion against the dominance of the Group. When they read a book, they embraced it utterly, talked of it, analyzed it, and soon the whole class was reading it. The themes of their current reading did not interest me, for the love of physical adventure that I'd so much cherished in my early reading had vanished, and the duels and knights and costume books and films bored me: my swashbuckling days were over. I did condescend to read the Anne Books of L. M. Montgomery and enjoyed them, especially the references to Anne's 'imagination.' So that was how one should be if one wished to be 'imaginative' – the Shirley Grave characteristics again – dreamy, poetic. In spite of my longing, I remained uncomfortably present within the world of fact, more literal than imaginative. I wanted an imagination that would inhabit a world of fact, descend like a shining light upon the ordinary life of Eden Street, and not force me to exist in an 'elsewhere.' I wanted the light to shine upon the pigeons of Glen Street, the plum trees in our garden, the two japonica bushes (one red, one yellow), our pine plantations and gully, our summerhouse, our lives, and our home, the world of Oamaru, the kingdom by the sea. I refused to accept that if I were to fulfil my secret ambition to be a poet, I should spend my imaginative life among the nightingales instead of among the wax-eyes and the fantails. I wanted my life to be the 'other world.' I thought often, gratefully, of the generous poets who had entered my world to write about Myrtle and our kingdom by the sea, mixing fact and fantasy in a poetic way that only made more vivid the events in Oamaru – 'sixteen years old when she died,' 'this was her book-shelf, this her bed . . .' That was indeed Myrtle, 'in her sixteenth year' as the obituary notices said. As for her 'bookshelf and bed,' that was indeed fantasy, for we girls slept all together top and tail in one bed, and the only bookshelf in the house was the one in the kitchen with Oscar Wilde, the dictionary, the Bible, God's Book, the Zane Grey Westerns, a book for children published by a tract society, *Stepping Heavenward*; *We are Seven*, which I always thought was meant to be our life story, for our family numbered seven; *The Last Days of Pompeii*; *The Vats of Tyre*; *To Pay the Price*; *From Jest to Earnest. John Halifax, Gentleman. Dr Chase's Book of Household Recipes* . . .

And just as I was inclined to submit to the Group's judgment in matters that they had experience of and I didn't – clothes, social life, dancing – I felt I had to submit to the poets in their conventions, their choice of words, and so I continued to write my verses replete with their dreams, dawns, and little old men with gray faces.

That year, also, I discovered the Ancient Mariner. One morning Miss Gibson came into the classroom and without any preliminary discussion sat at her table, opened a book, said in her 'announcing' voice, '"The Rhyme of the Ancient Mariner" by Samuel Taylor Coleridge' and began to read. She read the entire poem and said, 'Write an essay on the Ancient Mariner for next week,' then left the room. The lesson was over.

I had not known of the Ancient Mariner, and while Miss Gibson was reading, I listened, only half-understanding, to the story of the grim journey; and all else vanishing, I, too, was alone on the sea, living the living death, feeling the nearness of a seascape that was part of Oamaru. The sighting of the albatross was at the same time a farewell to the nightingales, for although I had never seen an albatross, Mother had talked of them and in our days at Fortrose and Waipapa she had sometimes pointed to distant seabirds and murmured, 'They may be albatrosses, kiddies.'

I did not comprehend the curse and the blessing of the mariner, only the journey and the suffering, and when in the last stanza Miss Gibson adopted her familiar preaching tone to read, 'He prayeth best who loveth best,' I resented her intrusion and the intrusion of the land and the landscape and the reduction of the mariner, seen through land-focusing eyes, from a man of mysterious grandeur even in guilt to a 'grey-beard loon.'

All that day I lived within the dream of the Ancient Mariner, a massive, inescapable dream that Miss Gibson had thrust upon us without explanation or apology, a 'pure' dream of that time on the sea in the embrace of weather that existed of itself without reference to people or creatures and their everyday lives of church, wedding guests, long-drawn-out tales. And of school, studying, playing basketball, swimming, writing poetry. And of milking cows.

For it was partly with the halcyon memory of the 'perfect' days 'before we shifted to Oamaru' and partly for the practical reason of supplying a growing family of people and cats with milk that Dad bought a cow from Luxons.

23

Scrapers and Bluey

The cow, a Jersey with big bones that suggested she might be a Jersey-Ayrshire cross and long, inward-curving horns, was already named Scrapers after her habit of scraping her hooves on the concrete floor of the byre. I found myself recruited to milk her as Dad would be too busy at work, Mum also was too busy, Isabel and June were too small, Bruddie too often sick. Nevertheless, June and Bruddie had learned to milk in case they might be called on to help. Scrapers was to be grazed on the reserve for a small fee, the reserve including all the pine plantations and the hill as far as the north end of town, which meant a long walk to find her, and so I formed the habit of taking Winkles, my cat, on my walk. Myrtle's black, fluffy cat, Big Puss, whose fur, like Old Cat's before her, now had a brown tinge of age and wear and tear, had given each of us our pet cat, each of a different color. Winkles was striped gray, named Winkles after her habit of blinking her eyes at me after one of those prolonged stares that cats like to direct at people.

Sometimes I'd milk Scrapers where she stood on the hill. Other times I'd bring her down to the small byre at the end of the garden, opening onto the bull paddock with a gate made from one end of Grandad's old iron bedstead. As I led Scrapers through from the reserve to the bull paddock, I'd put a rope over her horns and walk in front, and when we came to the creek, I'd jump across and, pulling at the the rope, try to persuade Scrapers to jump the creek. To my surprise, she readily accepted the routine but once or twice Winkles, in her eagerness, leapt into the creek, whereupon, again to my surprise, she swam strongly to the bank and climbed out. Then, when I had milked Scrapers, I'd return her to the hill and walk with Winkles to the top of the hill and, Winkles having now jumped onto my shoulder, I'd stare down at the familiar kingdom by the sea, listening to the waves crashing over the breakwater, seeing again Cape Wanbrow with its dark mass of pines and the ramble of buildings that were the Victoria Old People's Home, the town clock, the flour mill, the creek, the morgue, Thames Street, Reed Street, the Railway Station, the Engine Sheds, and, far out the North Road by the Boys' High, the tall chimney of the woollen mills. As I looked out at Oamaru, I'd compose a poem to write in my notebook later.

Now, at home, there was once again the sound of the separator being turned in the kitchen with the milk and cream spurting from their separate funnels into their separate bowls, the grinding of the wooden churn, the wood smooth and mellow with use, Mother singing as she patted the butter into shape with the ribbed butter pats and, as she 'scalded' the separator to clean it, intoning the word *scald* with an urgency, a hint of injury that she could not erase from its use in order to describe even a harmless act. There was milk to spare, a warmth of half-remembered infancy in the full, frothing-over bucket. This conscious attempt to re-create the 'old days' failed for me, because my 'old days' in Wyndham were of my being known as a thief, and I was thankful to escape, and because I was too much aware now of the present reality of my morning thorn-scratched school stockings, my milk-and-mud-splattered tunic and shoes, the sleepy dust in my morning eyes, the rush to get to school in time for assembly at nine o'clock, and the knowledge that after school I must go again in search of Scrapers. Even so, I knew that my time spent fetching, milking, and returning Scrapers and the precious moments gazing down at the kingdom by the sea, with Winkles rocking on her uneasy claw hold, my shoulder, were happy times as I was alone with my thoughts and my poetic dreams.

There were some days, however, when I was humiliated by not being able to understand the actions of Scrapers. I had no knowledge of the sexual life of cows, only that cows and bulls 'did it' standing up. Also, I had long ago closed my mind and forgotten all I had learned years ago about the workings of sex. Therefore, when Scrapers on some days began to dance around the paddock, refusing to let the rope be thrown over her horns, sometimes turning on me with horns lowered as if in anger, I felt sad that I was failing in my role as a milkmaid, for normally Scrapers and I were friends, and I was proud of the way she allowed me to milk her without a leg rope, anywhere on the hill, without her moving or putting her foot in the bucket. There was no answer at home to my confusion, for when I mentioned Scraper's strange behavior, Mother said casually, 'Leave her. I'll get Mr Luxon to take her.'

Apparently Mr Luxon had a bull 'out Weston way,' and so Scrapers would be taken to Weston, returning a few days later as her former placid self, and when eventually a calf was born, I was unable to understand the mutilation performed on the bull calves when they were a few months old and we, who had been feeding them, had grown fond of them. The operation was usually done at night, in secrecy, by a strange man who hurried away, leaving the bull calf hot-nosed and bleeding between its back legs. There was an element of ugliness, brutality, unhappiness, in the deed and in the casual way my parents answered my questions. I half knew and half didn't know. I knew that if Myrtle had been alive, she would have told me honestly with her mixture of fact and rumor, 'They've cut its thing off so it won't be a wild bull.'

The scar was on its balls: I could see it. And, for the life of me, I didn't know what balls were for, except perhaps to hold 'spunk.' I knew that the bull calf now became a bullock, growing to a different shape from a bull standing heavy and deep in the grass, more resembling a cow but with shriveled balls and a tiny, dangling thing.

The air of pretense about the matter infuriated me. I was usually left with the thought that a strange man had deliberately wounded our little bull calf, which we'd fed almost from the time it was born, putting our hand in its mouth and saying, 'Sook, sook, sook' to get it to start sucking, first in the bucket of yellow milk, then after a few weeks, of skim milk; that he'd deliberately wounded it and no one cared, not even our mother, only my sisters and I, because my brother already knew about the secret, and nobody was telling.

It was a different story with a heifer, an unexpected bonus because she could be sold. One, a pretty blue color, we decided to keep; and because she was a family animal, we could not call her any of the fancy names we were beginning to call any kittens that were not drowned at birth: the new calf was to be known as Bluey. Scrapers and Bluey. Scrapers and Bluey grazing there in the heartlands of my poetic world.

24
Faust and the Piano

There were few occasions when I earned money. In my primary school days, when I won a prize for a composition on 'My Visit to the Flour Mill,' I, influenced chiefly by the old schoolbooks and stories praising a mother's love, bought Mum a cup, saucer, and plate, Royal Doulton, on the advice of Mr Burton in the hardware and china shop. I also won small prizes for handwriting in the annual Agricultural and Pastoral Show, but none, to my disappointment, for my exhibits in the flower arrangement class where year after year I entered the section Gent's Buttonhole and once, daringly, the Miniature Garden. I had recently written a poem for the *Railway Magazine* for which I received one guinea. The poem, later included in Tom Mills's anthology of verse by New Zealand children, was my usual factual account of the natural world:

> On wintry mornings such as these
> when crystals decorate the trees
> when mists hang low upon the hill
> and frost is patterned on the sill . . .

After my introduction to the 'new' kind of music of the Schubert, Handel, and Mozart songs and the yearning to be able to play such music, I decided to use my guinea to pay for a term of piano lessons from Jessie C., who lived further up Eden Street with her mother and a white parrot in a spacious house, and who had offered to teach me music at a reduced rate, letting me practice on her piano, as we had none. Aunty Mima, the wife of Uncle Alex, the taxi driver, who lived on the South Hill and who had a piano, offered also to let me practice there on the weekends.

I confess that part of my joy at the prospect of learning music came from knowing that during the term when the teacher made her usual list of those pupils who 'learned' such things as dancing, music, elocution, I would at last be able to include my name, which had always been one of the two or three that, to their shame, 'learned' nothing.

Jessie C. was a small fair fluffy kind of person, perhaps in her thirties, a quiet contrast to her mother, who was known as the town gossip, for she and her parrot were able to glean facts and rumors that no one else knew. We could hear her parrot screeching during the day, when we'd say to one another, 'There's Ma discussing the latest with her parrot.' No one had ever seen or heard of a Mr C., and it was impossible to imagine one.

On my first visit to the house, Jessie showed me the piano in a carpeted, upholstered room full of knickknacks and patterns of roses, a cherished room as if a mother had lavished her love upon it as upon her children – well-fed, face-polished, warmly dressed with the black wood of the piano shining and the keys sparkling with darting graphs of light.

Jessie sat beside me on the padded 'duet' seat. 'Let me see your hands,' she said.

I showed her my cow-milking, fingernail-picked hands.

'You bite your fingernails, Jean.'

'I only pick them.'

'You'll never be able to play the piano unless you have nice fingernails.'

She held for my inspection her delicate hands with their beautifully curved and half-mooned nails. I had no half-moons. My shortcomings had been well catalogued in our comparing sessions at home: I had webbed fingers, I was not double-jointed, and I had no half-moons.

'You know of Middle C of course? Here's Middle C.'

I hadn't known of Middle C. At the end of the first lesson, when I'd been taught how to sit and how to place my hands and how the notes were named, Jessie gave me a small manuscript book and an instruction book for my homework. Dad had made it clear that there would be no money for examinations.

During the weeks that followed I learned to play 'Robin Adair,' ('What's this old world to me, Robin Adair?') and a number of short pieces of the raindrop birdhop tinkling variety. Then one day Jessie explained that it was important for me to have one first complete piece of music.

'A pianist always remembers her first piece of music,' she said dreamily, adding that she wanted me to have that special memory. She had already chosen the piece – 'Puck' – which I was to buy at Begg's, the music shop.

I went home. 'I have to buy a piece of music,' I said.

Mum looked apprehensive. 'I don't know whether your father . . .'

I milked the cow and waited for Dad to come home. I knew by heart the conversation that would follow. 'Dad, can I have some money to buy a piece of music?'

'What do you want a piece of music for? I told you learning the piano would cost more than you thought.'

'It's only a small piece. Ninepence.'

'I'm made of money, of course. Anyone would think I won Tatts every week.'

Here Mum would put in a word, saying how well I was doing on the piano, whereupon Dad, at the prospect of his daughter's future shining, would probably relent. It happened more or less according to the supposed script.

The next afternoon, on my way home from Begg's with the piece of music (which I'd already opened) in my hand, I met Jessie C. going downtown. I had no time to close the one new-smelling sheet of music that was 'Puck.' I felt ashamed and fearful that she had perceived my excitement. My embarrassment increased when at the next lesson she said slyly, knowingly, 'I saw you the other day with your first piece of music.'

I quickly learned to play 'Puck,' a staccato piece in F Major, meant to depict, I supposed, the frolicking of Puck:

> Over bush over briar
> through flood through fire
> I do wander everywhere
> swifter than the moon's sphere.

Then, once again, there was more music to be bought, this time a collection that, Jessie assured me, would last for years: Masterpieces of World Music. And once again Dad found the money for me to buy the music, a fat book packed with 'pieces' from all the great composers with few of whom I had any acquaintance, except those played in the School Music Festival –

'Schubert's Serenade,' 'Brahms' Lullaby,' 'Chopin's Minute Waltz.' I learned to play 'Londonderry Air' which I knew as 'O Danny Boy, the pipes the pipes are calling,' 'A Curious Story' by Stephen Heller. Then Jessie asked me if I knew of *Faust*. I didn't. She explained the story and introduced the 'Waltz' from the opera, which I learned to play. Next, Chopin's small Prelude in D, after which Jessie, who believed in milestones or keystones, said, 'My pupils usually give a recital to their parents when they have reached this stage.'

I knew of only one other pupil who had his lesson the same afternon as I – a hairy, dark-eyed high school boy named Rex, whose father worked in the clothing store, he, too, a hairy, dark-eyed man with large, pale hands adept at flipping over the bolts of material as he measured the required length. Rex would be leaving as I arrived, and each time we'd glance at each other, I with a new, mysterious sense of excitement and adventure. His eyebrows were thick as woolly-bear caterpillars above his dark face.

One afternoon, then, Mum put on her costume, her straw hat and navy gloves, and came up to Jessie's to hear me play the piano. I played 'Londonderry Air,' the waltz from the opera *Faust*, and the Chopin Prelude, and when I had finished, Jessie said to Mum, 'Jean's brilliant.'

This judgment pleased, confused, and frightened me with an intrusion of opinion and expectation that would now deny me the world of making music as a place of private escape. The performance of music was so present and public. My only escape was within myself, to 'my place,' within an imagination that I was not even sure I possessed, but where I hoped to avoid the praising, blaming scrutiny of others. Therefore, although I was proud of being thought 'brilliant,' I wanted to hide, and, noting this, Jessie said to Mum, using that identity-destroying third person, 'She's shy.'

During the remainder of the term I learned several pieces from the collection, going faithfully twice a week to practice and fearful lest Jessie or her mother or the parrot were listening at the door. I was never comfortable trying to practice in that comfortable room, and I hadn't realized how much I enjoyed the bare wooden floor at home, where scaters and earwigs came up through the cracks and cockroaches scuttled away into the dark. On Saturdays I went with June to practice on Aunty Mima's piano, which was old, out of tune, with the keys refusing to move from their bed. There, knowing that no one was listening, I spent the time 'tinkering' and experimenting after I'd played my pieces once to impress June with my cleverness.

Somehow the intrusion of judgment into my playing had blighted my interest. I began to make more mistakes, learning the pieces too quickly and then not being able to find my place in the music. I became self-conscious, with Jessie beside me on the duet seat, watching my nail-bitten, un-half-mooned fingers searching the keys. At the end of the term I finished my music classes with my last two pieces, the 'Shepherd Boy' ('like some vision of far-off time lonely shepherd boy') and 'To the Evening Star' ('O star of Eve'). Sometimes I felt lonely for the beautiful black shining piano and the warm, sealed room and the music, and now and again I'd see Rex, a part of the nostalgia, his music case banging against his long, hairy legs, walking up Eden Street to his lesson. We'd glance at each other, close as skin and distant as horizons.

25

Marking Time

My life centered on my schoolwork and my walks on the hill and reading and trying to write poetry. I was beginning to find that when I answered a question in school, the reaction of the class and the teacher was one of surprise, often of amusement. 'Jean's so original,' the teacher said one day, causing me once again to feel trapped by the opinion of others. I did not think of myself as original: I merely said what I thought. Yet an acknowledgment of an apparent 'difference' in my thinking seemed to fit in with the 'difference,' as I thought it to be, of my life at home with the dramatic terrifying continuing episodes of my brother's illness, the misunderstanding of it, the confusion of our parents trying to 'face' it, our brother's loneliness, my father's subdued withdrawal of 'control' over his daughters, our fervent promises not to 'stay out late, go with boys, drink, smoke' with the supposition that such an innocuous way of life would cure all; and when the idea of 'difference,' given to me by others in a time when I did not know myself and was hesitant in finding out, for I was not an introspective person, was reinforced by Miss Gibson's remark to Isabel, 'You Frame girls think you're so different from everyone else,' I came to accept the difference, although in our world of school, to be different was to be peculiar, a little 'mad.'

I believed always, however, in the politics of use, and now when I was asked about my reading and I (wearing the mantle of difference with pride) mentioned a novel few had heard of, the teacher would again say, 'Jean's so original.'

Therefore in an adolescent homelessness of self, in a time where I did not quite know my direction, I entered eagerly a nest of difference which others found for me but which I lined with my own furnishings; for, after all, during the past two years I had tried many aspects of 'being' – a giggling schoolgirl who made everyone laugh with comic recitations, mimicry, puzzles, mathematical tricks, such as 'Think of a number, double it,' attempts at ventriloquism; and now I was at home, with some prestige and fairly comfortable.

And while I struggled, enjoying my ambitions and my supposed 'difference,' out in the 'world,' far from New Zealand, the Nazi party was in power in Germany with speeches by Adolf Hitler being broadcast over the wireless. We mimicked his raving delivery, the Nazi salute, and the goose-stepping armies. I had little historical or political awareness. I knew only that Micky Savage and John A. Lee were 'goodies' while Forbes and Coates were 'baddies.' From time to time our history teacher had talked of the concept of 'purity of race' which, she said, was desirable. Intermarriage of races, she said, produced an inferior 'type,' citing the intermarriage of the Maoris and the Chinese. She spoke with pride of the 'purity' of the white race. Also at that time, by some subtle transmissions within the community, people who were Jewish were now identified as such and often spoken of in a slighting way. The word *nigger* was accepted as a description of African races and as a name for black cats, a color for shoe polish and items of clothing. And those people who were known to be 'half-caste' were spoken of as unclean.

This increased attention to 'purity of race' had come to our town no doubt by way of Nazi Germany and the British Empire, and there was much talk at school of *eugenics* and the possibility of breeding a perfect race. Intelligence tests became fashionable, too, as people clamored to find themselves qualified for the 'perfect race' and to find others who were not so qualified.

In our home, however, Mother, like the mother bird of the world, sprang always to defend all races and creeds (not quite; she condemned Roman Catholics) and colors as if they were her own 'youngkers' (our word for baby birds); while Dad, too, was without prejudice except toward the 'toffs' of the world and royalty.

And so, although at school we were often reminded of the distance of New Zealand from the rest of the world, the infection of Nazism did reach us in our town and we listened dutifully as our teacher painted some races evil, some good. One chapter in our history books, 'The Yellow Peril,' told of Eastern races and their evil designs on the West. Although we children had once chanted rhymes after all strange people, I remembered an elderly Chinese man walking by one day and our chanting at him and the baffled expression on his face when he looked at us, and I felt uneasy, as if I had done something I couldn't undo. Also, in the serials over the wireless and in Dad's Sexton Blake books, the villains were invariably described as 'yellow-skinned, slant-eyed, evil.'

Then, when during the year Dad was rushed to hospital with appendicitis and had for his neighbor a young Chinese man who, with his family, became family friends, we learned something of Chinese people. They came to visit us, and we visited them, and one day the young man brought us a beautiful plant, a narcissus growing, budding, and blossoming in water. We kept the plant on the sewing machine near the dining-room window, in the light, and whenever I looked at it I was aware of a new kind of beauty, a delicacy, which I tried to take and keep, for, in a way, my awareness of it helped to efface my growing consciousness of my body, the now-too-tight tunic often dirtied with cow muck and byre mud, the cobble-mended stockings coarse and thick, my frizzy tangle of red hair, which seemed to alarm everyone the way it naturally grew up instead of down, causing people to keep asking, 'Why don't you straighten it? Why don't you comb it flat, *make* it *stay* flat, put oil on it or something; *no one* else has hair like yours.' And no one had, except Fijian and African people in faraway lands. At school I was now called *Fuzzy*.

I had my fourteenth birthday. I could now use the whole of the Town Library and write to Dot's Senior Page. At school the Group's topic of conversation was new clothes – brassieres, corsets, corselets, each one being defined and the rules given for wearing each; the talk was of such urgency that I pleaded that evening, 'Mum, can I have a corset and brassiere?'

Mother, never having had either, said mildly, 'I'll not have you putting restrictions on your body.' O blind Mother, she did not even notice how tight my tunic had become across my developing breasts.

When Dad came home, I again brought up the subject, saying, 'All the girls at school are wearing them,' whereupon Dad made his familiar response, 'If all girls hopped to school, I suppose you'd hop, too!'

'That's different,' I said sourly.

But he was right, of course. It was just that the Group was so powerful I found myself wanting things simply because they made them seem to be such an urgent necessity. It's this or death. They were now taking lessons in ballroom dancing, looking forward to a time when they would be 'coming out.' They talked of their dancing partners at the Boys' High dances, the Bible Class socials, bike rides out 'The willows' with the Bible Class boys, and of what they would wear for their First Communion and Confirmation. I was ignorant of such ceremonies, as we did not belong to an established church, and when I heard one girl say to another, 'Are you being confirmed?' and the other girl reply, 'Yes, I'm being confirmed,' I felt sick with envy of the mystery and its urgency. How closely I listened to and studied the Group! I had no need to read Rafael Sabatini or Georgette Heyer to find myself in another world of costume drama: the other world was here, on a stone seat by the ivy-covered walls of Waitaki Girls' Senior High.

That year the speech contests were begun. I found the idea satisfying, for in all my early reading of school stories there had been a Speech Day, and I had felt the constriction of language at Waitaki, which was also a boarding school, where I had hoped to be able to use other words I had learned from my reading – midnight feasts in the *dorm*, being *gated*, being a member of the *Fifth Remove*, having *Hols* at the *seaside* (this was a problem because Oamaru *was* the seaside). Our speech subject was 'An Inventor or Explorer.' My heroes of exploration having been for many years Burke and Wills and Mungo Park, I chose Mungo Park, inventing many details, which I learned by heart and which to my delight and the delight of my parents, won First Prize.

And suddenly once again it was summer. Myrtle had now disappeared almost without trace. Sometimes when I tried to picture her, I found that her image had faded; I remembered only the white centipede scar on her knee and her golden hair, her *coiffure* done in the style of Ginger Rogers; her punches, pinches, back thumps; and my worry over what would become of her. She had been so fearless, adventurous, rebellious, a rule breaker, as my sister Isabel was growing up to be, defying the orders of adults, whereas I, still out of fear, obeyed them and even adapted myself to suit their opinion of me, my only place of rebellion being within, in an imagination that I was not even sure I possessed because, so far, no one had mentioned it.

That summer, perhaps not so inexplicably, we rediscovered Marguerite and her sister and brother and spent our time playing grown-up dolls who lived Hollywood-style lives with much loving, committing of adultery, divorcing, each of us propelling our tiny rose-pink Kewpie doll with its stuck-together legs, dressed in its elaborately made rayon gown, from room to room of the rayon-cushioned cardboard box mansions, and from bed to bed, with the appropriate gestures and dialogue.

They changed their clothes every few hours, with a glamorous gown for every occasion – their 'tea' gown, their 'sherry' gown. They danced, too, their bodies held close, after which they went out on the terrace to kiss and plan to 'go away together.' And the male characters, Nigel or Neil or Raymond, dressed always in evening dress, white front, cutaway coat, and a swath of black rayon for pants, as their legs, too, were stuck together, behaved always like 'wolves' who acted without ceremony when overcome by their desires. We graduated then, my sisters and I, from using Kewpies to using ourselves and, embarrassed by our daring, referred to our play, usually in our bedroom, as 'one of those games.' 'Let's play one of those games,' we'd say.

They lasted the summer when, for whatever reason, simply because the time had passed, a barrier came between us and the games, and we no longer referred to them or played them. Instead, we returned to our long walks in the gully and over the hill. Scrapers was now 'dry' and Bluey, in calf for the first time, was also dry but would be calved by the beginning of the school year.

Isabel and June and I were now all writing poetry and prose. I thought of Isabel's as the 'best,' for she covered a wide range of experience unknown to her, set in other countries, too, where she had never been. June's was, in my opinion, the most poetic, for she used the 'poetic' words, 'dream,' 'misty,' 'stars lost,' and so on, although her poems were vague, with few facts. My own poems, which usually had a satisfying ending, were in strict form, usually with the expected rhymes, and lacking the vague otherworldliness which I admired in June's poems and which I equated with the elusive 'imagination.'

My life had been for many years in the power of words. It was driven now by a constant search and need for what was, after all, 'only a word' – imagination.

26

Early Spring Snow

Another year at school with our class, the Lower Fifth, even smaller than our Fourth Form, although we shared some classes with the 'country and bus' girls who came from 4B. Once again the Group had control, although with the prospect of future examinations and the emphasis on studies, our small scholar's group had its own glory. There was W. and M., who was Miss Gibson's cousin and who came from a farming estate in the High Country, and I, Fuzzy. In spite of my father's urging, my competitive spirit was not strong, at least not so consuming as that of W., who wrote our marks and answers in a small notebook. We three usually worked on our own in mathematics where I became addicted to the solving of problems and the joyful experience of their neat solution.

Our class teacher, Miss Farnie, was small, ugly in the accepted sense, with her nose and chin too big, her face a blotchy red, her hair dark and scraggy. Her voice was soft yet clear, her eyes a calm gray, and her manner of teaching generally thought of as inspired with her passion both for English literature and for mathematics which, she explained to us, converting me entirely to the cause of mathematics, was a form of *poetry*. I believed her and therefore flourished in math.

It was she, too, who 'converted' me to Shakespeare, whom I'd previously thought was a bore. One day she walked into the room, opened our 'set' Shakespeare, *Macbeth*, and, with a witchlike voice that matched her appearance and swirling her black gown about her in a witchlike manner, began to read or drone,

> When shall we three meet again?
> In thunder, lightning, or in rain?
> When the hurlyburly's done,
> When the battle's lost and won.
> That will be ere the set of sun.

Miss Farnie then allotted parts to us (I was given First Witch) and asked us to read as witches would read, after which she announced that at the end of term we would perform the Sleep-Walking Scene and I was to be Lady Macbeth. I could scarcely believe my good fortune. Year after year it had been the girls from the Group who performed the major parts.

At home I practiced my role of Lady Macbeth. I read it in class, and I knew it was good. I dreamed of the coming performance. I began to take an interest in Shakespeare, in the wild Scottish moors and battles and battlements and the hauntings that were inseparable from the lives of the characters, and in the language used to describe the weather, the sky, the dark, to match the nightmare within the characters. My sisters and I read *Macbeth* at home, taking it to our hearts as we had taken the story of the Brontë sisters and using it as part of our conversation with one another, saying as Eden Street and the hill and the gully grew dark and the pigeons flew home to Glen Street:

> Now o'er the one half-world
> Nature seems dead, and wicked dreams abuse
> The curtained sleep.

As the weeks passed and I perfected my role of Lady Macbeth, gradually the demands of preparation for examinations invaded the class timetable, frivolities like acting were set aside, and no further mention was made of the performance of the Sleep-Walking Scene. It was hard for me to believe that something so memorable for me had been forgotten by the teacher and the class, and so I lost my chance to be Lady Macbeth. Even so I gained Shakespeare, whom I had longed to 'like' and to enjoy reading, as all the English teaching had given him unquestioned supremacy and I felt it would be impossible to think of being a writer if I didn't like reading Shakespeare; yet I'd found it impossible to pretend to admire him. Miss Farnie's approach had converted me.

It is strange to think of my life being lived as I then lived my 'real' life, so much within and influenced by English and French literature, with my daily adventures a discovery of a paragraph or a poem and my own attempts to write. It was not an escape in the sense of a removal from the unhappiness I felt over the sickness at home or from my own feeling of nowhereness in not having ordinary clothes to wear even to prove that I was a human being and there was a peopled world beyond home and school; there was no removal of myself and my life to another world; there was simply the other world's arrival into my world, the literature streaming through it like an array of beautiful ribbons through the branches of a green, growing tree, touching the leaves with unexpected light that was unlike the expected deserved habitual light of the sun and the seasons. It was the arrival, as of neighbors or relatives or anyone who belonged there and was at home, of the poets and the prose writers and their work at 56 Eden Street, Oamaru, 'the kingdom by the sea,' bringing their hosts of words and characters and their special vision.

Miss Farnie, in her praise for my weekly essays, so encouraged me that writing my essay became the highlight of my week, but as the reason for her praise was obscure to me, I tried to ensure its continuing with my emphasis on 'dreams, silver, mists, little old ladies, and little gray men.'

'Across the sea lies Shakespeare's isle, the land he loved and praised, the land that has seen happiness and sadness with her tired old eyes ...' I recall that opening sentence of one of my essays. I was painfully aware that I had no originality, no imagination, and I could not understand this sudden praise for my essays.

Those first few months in the Lower Fifth Form were happy. I rejoiced in my studies, encouraged by Miss Farnie's insistence not only that mathematics was poetry but also that poetry existed where few searched for it. This statement challenged me: out of a desire to be myself, not to follow the ever-dominant personalities around me, I had formed the habit of focusing in places not glanced at by others, of deliberately turning away from the main view, and I recognized in Miss Farnie someone with a skill in looking elsewhere or, looking at the general view, seeing an uncommon sight.

My memory of myself contains now myself looking outward and myself looking within from without, developing the 'view' that others might have, and because I was my body and its functions and that body was clothed during most waking hours in a dark gray serge tunic that I hated increasingly because it was far too tight now in the yoke, it was rough, scratchy material; and in long, black stockings with their sealing effect; and in blouses, pure white in summer, gray flannel in winter, all with cuffs buttoned tightly over my wrists and pointed collars closing with pearl buttons high upon my neck, completing the seal; and in the black shoes laced in complete capture of my feet; in the regulation gloves, hat, or beret; and, as a final imprisonment, in the red and black tie knotted around my neck and the green Gibson House Girdle also specially knotted around my waist, because of these clothes I saw myself as powerlessly in harness. Added to that view was my sisters' opinion of my 'figure' seen free and naked before the bedroom mirror, compared and contrasted with theirs and with the film stars and with the ideal, and although my opinion was important, I submitted readily to the general view. We concluded that we all had 'good' figures which, in our prancing before the mirror, we referred to in high-pitched American tones, 'Do you like my fig-ewer, Jebs?' (Jebs being short for Jebalus, who with May Cooney had been imaginary childhood friends.) My face, according to my sisters, was 'ordinary' except for my Shirley Temple dimples. We studied also the state of our skin and the number of blackheads or pimples on our face, the current influential advertisement being of a woman who could never wear 'off-the-face' hats because of her many hickies, which she successfully removed with a special soap or ointment.

There was also the question of 'personality.' One had to have 'personality.' I wasn't aware that I had any, although I had seized upon and embellished certain attributes that I may or may not have had. When Miss Farnie, having seen my poems in Dot's Page, said one day, 'You do write poetry, don't you, Jean?' and I blushed and looked embarrassed, and she said to the class, 'Jean's so shy,' I seized this (already given by Jessie C., the music teacher) as a welcome, poetic attribute and made shyness a part of my 'personality.'

Looking out at the world, then, from my position of physical discomfort, I felt restricted to the point of being nastily bad-tempered at my task of milking Scrapers and Bluey, for Bluey and Scrapers had calved and both cows were 'in milk.' I began to write a diary, agreeing with the convention and aware that diarists began 'Dear Diary'; yet thinking such a form of address to be absurd, I compromised by writing 'Dear Mr Ardenue,' Mr Ardenue being pictured as a kindly old man with a long, gray beard and 'smiling' eyes, who ruled over the Land of Ardenue, which I celebrated in a poem. Where before I had written most of my verse about the world around me, I now focused on the Land of Ardenue, which I could people as I wished. The important consistent characters were Mr Ardenue, the ruler of the kingdom; the Sea-Foam Youth Grown Old, who came to mind one day as I watched the waves breaking and the foam on the beach turn quickly brown; the Scholar Gypsy, from Arnold's poem, the Scholar Gypsy being perhaps my first 'love,' my ideal man, reawakening my early feeling for gypsies and my kinship with Old Meg Merrilees and my special feeling for all beggars and swaggers passing through town in the dark, glistening night and prisoners, again at night, in the moonlight, longing for freedom yet possessing a special freedom like that of the Scholar Gypsy. Having read Arnold's poem for the first time that year, I was able to weave my dreams of the future about his life both as a scholar and a free wanderer, shy, seldom glimpsed, at home with the natural world of wood, weather, and sky and season.

There were a few unlikely characters in Ardenue, mostly invited there to satisfy my strong attraction to ordinary everyday objects that might in the end become extraordinary: *The Dishes I Washed*. That was how they were known and how they were greeted in each entry of my diary. There were also *The Little Golden Ladies of New Zealand*, installed in Ardenue under the continued influence of Mother's poetic interests and the fondness of her and her poetic friends (she corresponded with one or two people who wrote poetry) for writing of *Kowhai Blossoms*. Indeed, one of Mother's friends had lately published a book of poems entitled *Kowhai Blossoms*. I, impressed, read it, noting from the foreword that the author, true to the growing tradition, was blind, a fact that Mother cherished, using it once again to demonstrate that handicaps could be overcome and glory achieved. My own *Little Golden Ladies of New Zealand* were some fallen kowhai blossoms that I saw in a Oamaru garden. I seized also the much-loved poplar trees, and each pine plantation was transplanted in Ardenue, and the moon that I watched each evening as it rose over the sea. In the creation of Ardenue I gave a name and thus a certainty to a new inner 'My Place.'

So tightly encased were we girls in our senior high school tunics that I am surprised at the ease with which in August of 1939 the first menstrual blood was able to find its way out of my body. I should have been prepared for the escape; I was not. I'd forgotten the faraway time of Myrtle and her 'monthlies.' I didn't even know what to call menstruation, for 'monthlies' was a word of the past, out of date, and the girls at school talked of being 'unwell.'

I was nearly fifteen when I woke that morning to find blood between my legs. Panic seized me. I ran from the bedroom into the dining room and stood in the place where Mother herself stood in time of crisis – that honored place in the light of the dining-room window, by the sewing machine, where we had been warned not to stand should there be a storm and danger of lightning.

'There's blood between my legs,' I said tremulously.

'It's the monthlies,' Mother said.

Gradually my memory returned. I had forgotten, however, the reasons and the mechanics that I knew so well at eight years old. Mother cut an old bath towel into rectangular strips, giving me one to pin back and front to my singlet, for bought sanitary towels were unheard of in our household.

'It will show,' I said, looking unhappily at the bulk.

'No, it won't show,' Mother lied valiantly.

I knew it showed. For the remaining years at school I suffered those bulky strips of toweling with the blood seeping through so that by the end of the day, if I bent my head toward my desk, I caught the smell of stale menstrual blood, and realizing that others would also smell it, I felt unceasing shame. The bulk and the stink and the washing of the towels became a haunting distaste. I did not even experience the coveted prestige of feeling 'unwell' and being sent to 'lie on the bed in the prefects' room,' where L., the class artist, had often to go, her Lady of Shalott face deadly pale.

That month of August there was a late, unexpected snowstorm, the kind that kills the newborn lambs in the high country, and even Oamaru, the kingdom by the sea, had a few days of deep snow. The timing of the snowfall, following so closely my shock of being bathed in blood, had a literary perfection not thought of as being a part of the untidiness of living and a shape, drawing together the past of Grimm's Fairy Tales and the repeated incidence there of blood upon the snow as a catastrophic or miraculous moment deciding the direction of the character's future, touching, too, my present life as a chrysalis-bound schoolgirl. Because I could feel yet not express the pattern, I wrote two poems that I sent to Dot. 'Early Spring Snow' was in my usual style, beginning:

A cloud of softly whirling flakes has o'er the hillside bent.
The violets murmur drowsily steeped in their fragrant scent.
A wintry wind has wailed all night a tale of lone lament.

We had been studying William Cowper's poem, 'To Mary':

The twentieth year is well-nigh past,
Since first my sky was overcast;
Ah would that this might be the last!

The other poem, 'The Blackbird,' read:

Surely O surely the message is Spring
with snowdrops in delicate white . . .

And so on. Concluding with:

The whole world awakened and thrilled to the song
no more was the bleak hillside cold,
for nodding and whispering in garments of sheen,
a crocus began to unfold.

To my delight, Dot praised both poems, using 'The Blackbird' as the Poem of the Week, a place normally reserved for poems by 'real' poets. I was annoyed that she changed 'gay' blackbird to 'blythe' blackbird, for I thought 'blythe' too clumsy. Over the years I remember my irritation over the change of my chosen word, just as I remember Myrtle's pressure to change 'touch' to 'tint.'

I had my fifteenth birthday. Birthday parties were unknown luxuries in our home, and the day passed more or less as usual. At home I still practiced my Lady Macbeth speech, more aware now of its meaning – 'Here's the smell of the blood still. All the perfumes of Arabia will not sweeten this little hand.'

My own hands were strong, from the exercise of milking the cows.

The land of Ardenue continud to absorb me, and I dreamed again and again of the Scholar Gypsy, especially as Miss Farnie had recommended a book, *Towers in the Mist*, by Elizabeth Goudge – a tale of Oxford University that captured the whole class, including the Group, with its romantic descriptions of Oxford and the scholars: 'Seen by rare glimpses, pensive and tongue tied,/In hat of antique shape, and cloak of grey,/The same the gypsies

147

wore . . .' (I thought of Old Meg's 'chip hat.') 'Have I not pass'd thee on the wooden bridge,/Wrapt in thy cloak and battling with the snow . . ./Turn'd once to watch, while thick the snowflakes fall,/The line of festal light in Christ-Church Hall . . .'

Towers in the Mist made Oxford and the Scholar Gypsy even more desirable, and yet I felt an uneasiness, almost a disappointment, that Miss Farnie, with all English literature to reveal to us, thought so highly of a book where the writing reminded me of L. M. Montgomery and the Anne books, lacking a solidity, a factual concreteness in the midst of the misty vagueness. Certainly it was gentle writing, with all the green and gold and little old men and women, the dreams, and most of the vocabulary that I still thought necessary to poetry.

But Miss Farnie was a teacher of her time, middle-aged, unmarried, as far as we knew, with the inevitable rumors of her 'boy' being killed in the Great War and her journey of a lifetime 'home' to England completed and the memories carefully preserved in the 'slides' that she showed the class as a special treat – the English lanes, the country cottages, the ruins, the castles, the universities, ah, the universities, Oxford and Cambridge . . . the towers in the mist . . . she passing on her dreams, which we made part of ours, for there was much preoccupation now with university examinations, with degrees and careers, and some of the girls with older brothers and sisters at university told of their experiences, while I, investigating the world of literature, discovered that many of the poets had been to university.

I have often wondered in which world I might have lived my 'real' life had not the world of literature been given to me by my mother and by the school syllabus, and even by the death of Myrtle. It was my insistence on bringing this world home, rather than vanishing within it, that increased my desire to write, for how else could I anchor that world within this everyday world where I hadn't the slightest doubt that it belonged? Oamaru, the kingdom by the sea. Did I not already know people in Oamaru who had been 'trodden down' by the 'hungry generations'? And did we not have the natural ingredients for literature – a moon, stars ('Pale star, would I were steadfast as thou art'), sea, people, animals, sheep, and shepherds ('Go, for they call you, shepherd, from the hill'). We had skylarks dipping and rising above the hill ('Hail to thee, blithe spirit!') and pigeons and goldfinches and wax-eyes clamoring to have their say above the nightingales . . .

In early September of that year, in the midst of a concentration of characters from fiction and poetry, and inhabitants of the Land of Ardenue, in a setting of blood and snow, that storm and that lightning which I had defied by standing near the light of the dining-room window, with the sky beyond, struck not only our house but also all the houses in Eden Street, in Oamaru, New Zealand, the world, in the outbreak of the Second World War.

27

'That's Not You, Jasper.'

Had I been a city, the shock of war would have torn apart all buildings, entombing the population, or as after a volcanic eruption there might have been an overflow of numbness, like lava, preserving all in a stone mask of stillness and silence. I had never felt so shocked, so unreal. I knew that war happened in history and in places far away, in other nations; that my father had 'been to the war'; that some of the stories I most loved featured young soldiers 'on their way to the wars' or wounded old soldiers coming 'home from the wars.' I had relished Miss Lindsay's reading of 'Ode on the Death of the Duke of Wellington' and the battles of the time of Arthur: 'So all day long the noise of battle rolled . . .' And year after year in the School Journal I had read:

> In Flanders field the poppies blow
> Between the crosses, row on row
>   That mark our place; and in the sky
>   The larks, still bravely singing, fly
> Scarce heard amid the guns below . . .

In the Anzac Commemoration at the Waitaki Boys' High School Hall of Memories I had heard Mr Milner proclaiming the British Empire's glorious deeds in battle and sung, feelingly, without translation of the scene into one of undue horror:

> O Valiant Hearts, who to your glory came
> Through dust of conflict and through the battle-flame;
>   Tranquil you lie, your knightly virtue proved,
>   Your memory hallowed in the Land you loved . . .

I knew of the pacifist belief of Mother's religion, that two of her brothers had been conscientious objectors in the First War and imprisoned for their refusal to kill. I tried to imagine the people I knew in Oamaru – the Walsh boys, the Easton boys, the Luxons, even Jack Dixon, becoming characters in this new story and with knapsack or kit bag setting out cheerfully for the war. I had honestly believed that the days of war were over.

Recovering a little from the shock and feeling an inconsolable sadness and disillusionment, I turned once again to the poets who, I believed, were rightly described by Shelley as 'the unacknowledged legislators of the world.' I felt, too, that 'poetry redeems from decay the visitations of the Divine in Man.' I felt that to know which way the winds of the world were blowing, to gain knowledge of human behavior, of the working of the human mind, I had only to study the world's poetry and fiction. Just as the poets had taught me of death and included my own experiences in their writing, so they would teach me about war.

Oamaru and New Zealand appeared suddenly to be seized by a kind of madness as if the Declaration of War were an exciting gift. There was a flurry of anticipation in our home as both my father and my brother thought of being soldiers. Dad searched out the 'puttees,' which he'd brought home from *his* war and which had lain untouched in an old suitcase. 'My puttees,' he said with a new affection, demonstrating how they were used by winding them over his trouser legs. 'Keep out the mud of the trenches,' he said knowledgeably. He'd seldom talked of the trenches before. The word was used only by Mum to explain why Dad was so often either sad or angry, 'Your father fought in the trenches, kiddies,' and by us at primary school in scoring points of prestige, 'My father fought in the trenches.'

There was a kind of war fever in the town. Young men hurried to enlist with few questioning the duty to 'rally round to help the Mother Country.' Flags appeared on buildings. The wireless played Rule Britannia, and even Mother, the pacifist, clenched her fist and said, 'We'll show Hitler!' The newspaper issued a large map complete with flags with the markings of the Maginot Line and the Siegfried Line and other places and the instruction *Flag the Movement of the Allied Forces from Day to Day*, as if the affair were a game. And both Dad and Bruddie went downtown to join the army with Dad returning as a member of the newly formed National Reserve, complete with uniform, and Bruddie, who was unfit, as a member of the Home Guard with a porkpie hat gathered from somewhere. At school there were subtle shiftings of prestige as girls previously ignored were found to have fathers with the rank of colonel or major or brothers in the First Echelon. Dad had been a corporal, a signaler and stretcher-bearer in the First World War by which name it was now officially known, its greatness being finally in doubt.

I went about my daily tasks at home – milking the cows, often sharing the job with Bruddie, taking my 'turn' at riding Dad's bike downtown for the messages, trying to maintain my school tunic now scratched and torn by the wire fence of the hill and the bull paddock; arguing, comparing, contrasting with my sisters, helping as little as possible with the housework but occasionally cooking in an experimental way my 'discovery' of mock whitebait: for wartime was the time of 'mock' food, with the very notion causing a consternation of betrayal in our home similar to the news of permanent waves.

The poetry that I then explored was generally an easy kind of poetry made more attractive for me by the usual handsome photograph of the young poet in his soldier's uniform. Unable to face the City of Dreadful Night 'As I came through the desert thus it was . . .,' which was the reality of war, I turned to the shallow acceptance of glorifying the war dead, with Rupert Brooke as my hero and 'If I should die think only this of me' setting the tone. And how quickly we learned the new language of war! Men suddenly became known as 'boys,' 'our boys,' returned to childhood with a license to kill. Our boys, the brave. At school we talked familiarly of echelons, quislings, fifth columnn, the blitz, the names of planes and places; and in my poetry I wrote:

> Brown soft brown in the tall gold grass
> a skylark rested, and far away
> the song of pride in the men who pass
> dreaming of war in a boyish way,
> tumbled its notes to a quiet street.
> O surely, surely the day is sweet
> when the soldiers march!

The poem of several verses concluded with:

> When they, the brave, have gone have gone
> and flowers weep with the lovely dew,
> then, little bird, be glad, sing on,
> sing and the world shall list to you.
> And we shall laugh, yet creeps a tear

and clutches the heart a silent fear
When the soldiers march.

That poem and many others in a similar vein were printed in the local newspaper, and I was not ashamed of them as I am now. I was humanly naïve and ungrown, using to describe a dire event the latest 'poetic' words in my vocabulary – *dreaming, boyish, sweet* – with the old standbys – *lovely, little, laugh* ... I had good tutors, you see – Rupert Brooke – 'Laughed in the sun and kissed the lovely grass ...' Flowers, dew, stars, skies ... the words ruled, you see; they held the keys of the kingdom, and I did not realize until I had spent a few more years growing and observing that the kingdom which glorified those words was as much a prison as my gray serge tunic and knotted tie and lace-up black shoes.

The remainder of that year is memorable only as the continuing nightmare of war and certain nightmares at home, alleviated once again by the solace of the seasons, the weather, reading and writing poetry, learning passages by heart, and receiving a present. I gave my speech on Speech Day – 'A Character from Literature' Silas Marner (the little old man), making him a romantic character. I won the Speech Prize. At the end of the year I was asked to choose my class prize, and once again Mother's influence showed in my choice of Longfellow, a handsome book with illustrations shrouded in tissue paper and, uncovered, revealing a bronzed handsome Hiawatha, more handsome than Rupert Brooke, carrying Minnehaha in his arms:

Over wide and rushing rivers
In his arms he bore the maiden

Then there was the present, with Dad giving me five shillings to buy myself a book for Christmas, the first book I had ever bought.

I went to Jeffrey and Smith's and asked for my chosen book, *Lavengro*, by George Borrow, because it combined many of my interests. Old Meg the gypsy, the Scholar Gypsy, it contained also the passage that I'd read often in our schoolbooks and that I longed to possess, to read again and again, especially now in 1939 in the midst of war: the pasage beginning, 'That's not you, Jasper ...' and ending, 'Life is sweet, Jasper. There's day and night, Jasper, both sweet things. There's sun, moon and stars, brother, all sweet things, there's likewise a wind on the heath. Who would wish to die?'

28

University Entrance

I think of the remaining years at school as part of the nightmare of the war, the daily casualty lists, the hymns and Bible readings in school assembly:

> Eternal Father strong to save
> whose arm hath bound the restless wave . . .
> O hear us when we cry to thee
> for those in peril on the sea . . .

and

> Fight the good fight with all thy might . . .
> Christ is thy strength and Christ thy right.

and

> Peace perfect peace in this dark world of sin
> the blood of Jesus whispers peace within.

I recall the seriousness and fervor of my singing, the (then innocently) sexual languor of the many hymns steeped in blood, such hymns being favorites with the girls, most of whom in the past year or two had acquired a new relationship to blood, made strange by the repeated reference to the spilling of blood in wartime, and the everlasting preoccupation with blood in a country that based its economy on the killing and eating of farm animals.

I began my year in the Upper Fifth Form with Miss Macaulay as my form teacher and Miss Farnie still my mathematics teacher, with another bursary to help to pay for books. This was the year of the University Entrance Examination. It was also the year of the country's centenary with celebrations to be held in Wellington and a party from the school arranging to go for educational purposes, these being the chief point of the argument of my sisters and me when we pleaded to be able to go with the school party. Once again we were infected by the desire to belong in a school activity, when year after year we'd had to refuse the visit to Mount Cook (which I have still not visited), camping trips, and so on. Also, we pointed out to our parents that we'd have our free railway ticket, and with so many relatives in Wellington there'd be no need for us to be 'billeted.' The cost would be slightly more than an allowance of pocket money each, although we never had pocket money. When the list was made, however, we tasted the rare glory of inclusion, partly because the prospect of another 'Exhibition' had prompted Mum and Dad to remember with nostalgia the South Seas Exhibition in Dunedin:

'When Myrtle and Bruddie were little and Aunty Grace and Uncle Andy lived at Balclutha. And Myrtle and Bruddie had candy floss . . .' The candy floss was always mentioned as if it were the sweetest kind of uncomplicated happiness known only then, in the days of the Dunedin Exhibition, after the Duke and Duchess of York and the Prince of Wales had toured the country (O the lovely Prince of Wales!) after the king's furniture had been paid for, and there was no longer danger of the king's representative coming to inspect the iron bed and the wooden kerb and the dining table with the four morris chairs and the sofa and the oval hearth rug . . . Oh, they were heaven days 'when Myrtle and Bruddie were little . . .' 'So be sure to have some candy floss,' Mum said. 'You may never have another chance. They only have it at Exhibitions and suchlike . . .'

The journey in the ferry was rough with all the girls seasick and Miss Lindsay, one of the chaperoning teachers, also sick. During the night she had held my head as I vomited again and again while she reminded everyone, 'Go with the motion of the boat, go with the motion of the boat,' and when morning came with its awful sea green light there was Miss Lindsay, her face gray green as she sat miserably on the stairs, pointing out the geographical features of the approaching Wellington harbor, for 'after all, girls, this is an educational visit!'

The party, billeted at Newtown school, carried out its plans while we three girls, separated from the others, discovered new aunts and uncles and cousins 'on Mother's side,' while we spent our two days at the Exhibition and our pocket money by enjoying the attractions of the Fun Fair and the Hall of Mirrors, riding the

Ghost Train, and finally having our handwriting analyzed by a *gypsy*, who warned me what I already knew, that my 'personality' was in trouble, that I was too shy, too self-conscious.

Returning from the Exhibition, we wrote the inevitable essay. I wrote about the pleasures of the educational and industrial courts. We had tasted candy floss (surreptitiously in case we were 'seen,' as Waitaki girls were forbidden to eat in public), and partly sensing our parents' use of it as a memory of vanished happiness, we proclaimed ourselves unimpressed by it; we preferred, we said, to eat something more substantial. I know that Mother's expectations were disappointed when she realized that she could not re-create her old memories from our new ones, that the halcyon time of 'when Myrtle and Bruddie were little' was out of reach, had even been canceled.

Nevertheless, June and Isabel and I had our own kind of candy floss: that educational visit was always remembered as a time of great freedom and fun when, for a time, I even forgot the war – and the University Entrance Exam.

Once again in Oamaru we faced the casualty lists, the rumors, the morning hymns, the reference to the exam. I returned also to my life within the poetry and prose I was discovering. Reading a poem acknowledged to be 'great' (such as 'Ode on the Intimations of Immortality'), I was pleased to be 'moved to tears,' as I felt that to be so affected helped to seal the greatness of the poem, and each evening when I wrote in my diary, I felt a certain pride if I were able to write to Mr Ardenue, 'Today I wept in class when we were reading . . .' naming the poem or prose. My weeping was not audible nor, as far as I knew, noticeable, although I did hope that the teacher might perhaps glance my way, see me wiping away a tear, and think, 'Ah, there's Jean, so moved by poetry, so poetic, so imaginative . . . a real poet herself . . .' I had no indication that the teacher thought such things . . . and still the longed-for imagination eluded me.

With the concentration on the coming exams and their very name – *University Entrance* – there was talk among the girls about their future university courses and of life at university, which some even dared (to my alarm at their familiar tone) to call *Varsity*. Towers in the Mist, the Scholar Gypsy, Wordsworth's Sonnet on King's College Chapel, Cambridge, Jude the Obscure and the towers of Christminster, Shelley, Byron, Matthew Arnold, now combined as a dream to replace the dream of Hollywood, of dancing, singing and the Big Time among the stars, although these departing dreams did flare occasionally with the arrival of new adolescent singing stars – Judy Garland, Deanna Durbin, and the search through New Zealand for a *New Zealand Deanna Durbin* with hundreds of girls trilling 'Il Bacio' ('Softly dawns upon me, dawns upon me morning's laughing rays . . . returning yes returning . . .') and the 'Pipes of Pan' ('Come follow follow follow the merry merry pipes of Pan . . .'), I experiencing and making use of the reflected glory of having my aunt's two nieces (aunt by marriage, alas!) reach the provincial final, only to give way to the heralded New Zealand's *own* Deanna Durbin, June Barson. From Auckland of course.

Gradually I was acquiring an image of myself as a person apart from myself as a poet, and in my reading I identified most easily with the stoical solitary heroine suffering in silence, the 'plain Jane' content to love the strong, inarticulate hero who was easily beguiled by the flashily beautiful woman but who turned always in the end (regretfully too late) to the shadowy shy woman he had failed to notice. I saw myself as a 'background' person watching, listening. I was not Becky Sharp; I was Emma. Yet I was also Tess and Marty South, as I had once been Anne of Green Gables and Charlotte Brontë (Isabel being Emily, and June Anne). I was Maggie Tulliver and Jane Eyre and Cathy. And when I could find no heroine to become, I was myself simply adoring the heroes – Jude the Obscure, Raskolnikov, Brutus, rather than Mark Antony, whom *everyone* liked. There were the film heroes, too – Robert Donat, Laurence Olivier, Clark Gable. My lasting heroes were, naturally, the poets, French and English – Daudet, Victor Hugo, Keats, Shelley, Wordsworth, Rupert Brooke, Yeats (in his early phase of 'old men admiring themselves in the water' and 'the cloths of Heaven'), most of the poets from my fourth-form prize *The Golden Book of Modern English Poetry* and from our *Shakespeare to Hardy* – and the prose writers, Dostoevski, Hardy, the Brontës, George Eliot, Washington Irving, E. B. Lucas, Sir Thomas Browne.

And Shakespeare.

I knew of few New Zealand writers, only Katherine Mansfield, Eileen Duggan, William Pember Reeves, Thomas Bracken, all of whom I thought of as 'belonging' to my mother, and because I did not think of myself as belonging to her world, I had no desire to share 'her' writers. Her Longfellows and Twains and Whittiers, yes, but not writers that she or her parents or grandparents might have known. For our speech that year, 'An Author,' I chose Francis Thompson, whom I had 'discovered' for myself, and I felt curious when one member of the class, choosing Katherine Mansfield, was commended by the teacher for choosing a New Zealand writer when none of our English studies even supposed that a New Zealand writer or New Zealand existed.

My last years at school were also busily practical. I was a member of the B basketball team and eventually became captain. I gained my Elementary Certificate in Life Saving. I was a keen diver. Seized by a longing to play tennis, I used the pound note from my 'marks' for poems in the Children's page of the *Truth* to pay for the frame of a tennis racquet, which someone Dad knew had offered to string for a reduced rate, but when the racquet was complete, my shame was overwhelming when I found the strings were black instead of cream. I pronounced the racquet 'funny.' I was not brave enough to parade my racquet in all its difference, and the one day I brought it to school, I was certain that 'everyone noticed it,' and from then it remained unused, on top of the wardrobe beside the two big sleeping dolls, one dressed in pink, the other in blue, the clothes made by a friend of Aunty Isy and the dolls given to June and Isabel when they felt too grown-up to play with them, which was just as well, for they were warned that the clothes were 'knitted specially by an old woman' and must be taken care of . . . The unused racquet and the unused dolls stayed there until my sister June had children who used them without fear of difference or of harming the 'specially knitted' dolls' clothes. By then, the friend of Aunty Isy, and Aunty Isy herself were dead.

That year our cats were stricken with what must have been feline enteritis, and one by one they died. I seized on Winkles' death to write an elegy, which I sent to the Mail Minor under my nom de plume, Amera. I was prepared to make use of everything in the interests of poetry, like a bird lining its nest, an apt comparison, for a new interest now occupied members of the Group, their influence still unbroken and powerful in the classroom – the preparation of their 'box,' a term new to me. Instead of being given isolated birthday and Christmas presents, they were now collecting household items, such as linen, cutlery, china, with each addition discussed and described in detail. No matter how distant I felt myself to be from them, I could say that they and I were engaged in similar pursuits – all collecting materials for the future we hoped to have, they their household goods, I my experiences and fictional characters. When I say that I 'seized on' Winkles' death to write an elegy, I could say that I also felt an obligation to the poets who had written about Myrtle's death, to share the death of Winkles and my feelings about it, and that all experiences collected for the future were not for individual use only like household linen and cutlery, but for common use within a stream which, I was beginning to sense, might be called history.

When I wasn't able to plead the excuse of 'studying for exams,' I still milked the cows, the duty now shared with Robert and June; walking the hills in search of Bluey and Scrapers, gazing out at the harbor and the sea, the Cape, familiar sights, placing in my mind that tiny, windowless building that we still knew as the morgue; the park where Wirth's Circus and Sixpenny Zoo camped each year and where we, desperate to see a circus and never seeing it, tried to peep under the tent; the tree-lined street; missing Winkles balanced on my shoulder, but consoling myself with thoughts of the Sea-Foam Youth Grown Old, the Scholar Gypsy, Mr Ardenue, and all the characters from the fiction I was reading; wondering about and dreading the future, for in spite of my dream of university, I knew that I would have to train as a teacher, for teachers, unlike university students, were paid.

Our parents had receded from our lives. We discussed school affairs with them, asked them for money for this and that, and either were given it or not. We were impatient with their ignorance of school subjects. Aware now that Mother had turned increasingly to poetry for shelter, as I was doing, I, with an unfeelingness based on misery of feeling, challenged the worth of some of her beloved poets, aware that my criticism left her flushed and unhappy while I felt a savage joy at her distress. I had begun to hate her habit of waiting hand and foot, martyrlike upon her family. When I was eager to do things for myself, Mother was always there, anxious to serve. I now felt the guilt of it, and I hated her for being the instrument of that guilt. Her invisible life spent on her distant plane of religion and poetry, her complete peacefulness, angered me just as I knew it angered my father, who sometimes tried to taunt her to show anger or accepted selfishness or any unsaintly feeling that might bring disapproval from the Christ she tried so hard to please. At such times Mother would flush slightly and, pursing her lips, begin to sing softly:

> When He cometh when He cometh
> to make up His jewels,
> all His jewels, precious jewels
> His loved and His own.

or the chosen song of the Christadelphians, 'Mine eyes have seen the glory of the coming of the Lord,' the 'Battle Hymn of the American Republic,' or the other favorite, 'Zion's King shall reign victorious,/He shall set his people free ...' which, sung to the tune of the German National Anthem, prompted my father to taunt, 'There you are, singing the *German* National Anthem.'

Our home was seldom happy now. The festivals that we cherished had lost most of their joy with our growing up. Our brother, who had discovered alcohol and made a strong brew of beer in the washhouse copper, was in a turmoil of adolescent confusion and depression at his sickness, having to bear Dad's continued belief that 'he could stop the fits if he wanted to' and Mother's urging, 'Be strong, Bruddie, be strong. Many of the great men of the world had epilepsy,' and unable to fit into this expected role of superboy, sometimes he was brought home after being found lying in the gutter outside the billiard room. Isabel tried to make him sign a pledge, 'A pledge I make/no wine to take ...' Various people of the town who had promised him help with work had failed to honor their promises. Garfield Todd of the Church of Christ was one who did help.

And so day by day we polished Dad's buttons on his National Reserve uniform, read the casualty lists, accepted the new words of war, listened to the BBC news, flagged the movement of the Allied Forces. And at school the University Entrance exam came and went, and I passed, remembering the exam now chiefly for the two guineas which it cost to enter and which I struggled to get, with my father insisting that I should leave school. A few years later my first published story in the *Listener*, 'University Entrance,' earned me that sum, confirming for me once again the closeness, the harmony, and not the separation of literature (well, a simple story!) and life.

29

Imagination

Where in my earliest years time had been horizontal, progressive, day after day, year after year, with memories being a true personal history known by dates and specific years, or vertical, with events stacked one upon the other, 'sacks on the mill and *more on still,*' the adolescent time now became a whirlpool, and so the memories do not arrange themselves to be observed and written about, they whirl, propelled by a force beneath, with different memories rising to the surface at different times and thus denying the existence of a 'pure' autobiography and confirming, for each moment, a separate story accumulating to a million stories, all different and with some memories forever staying beneath the surface. I sit here at my desk, peering into the depths of the dance, for the movement is dance with its own pattern, neither good nor bad, but individual in its own right – a dance of dust or sunbeams or bacteria or notes of sound or colors or liquids or ideas that the writer, trying to write an autobiography, clings to in one moment only. I think of the times we used to sit by the Rakaia river, watching the branches and trunks of trees, the dead cattle and sheep, swept suddenly from the main stream to the many whirlpools at the side where, their force no less swift, they stayed a moment only before being drawn down down toward the center of the earth.

I struggled with the events of those last years at school. I felt bewildered, imprisoned – where would I go? What if my parents died suddenly? What was the world like? How could the world be at war? I asked myself that old question which haunted me as a child, Why was the world, why *was* the world? And where was my place? I had those recurring dreams of being grown up and returning to school only to be told, What do you think you're doing here? You're grown up.

My sisters and I immersed ourselves in our reading and studying. To pass the long, hot summer, we began our 'novels': mine was

The Vision of the Dust from Chesterton's poem 'The Praise of Dust':

> Rich white and blood-red blossom; stones,
> > Lichens like fire encrust;
> A gleam of blue, a glare of gold,
> > The vision of the dust.

Isabel's title was *Go Shepherd* from 'The Scholar Gypsy'; June's, *There is Sweet Music* from 'The Lotos-Eaters.' We did not get beyond the first few chapters of our novels. We continued to send our poems to the *Mail Minor*, the *Truth*, and *Dot's Little Folk*, and one week memorable for me saw another of my poems, 'Blossoms,' made Poem of the Week, and the other, 'The Crocus,' also praised by Dot, whose remarks were: 'Thank you for the poems, Amber Butterfly. They show poetic insight and imagination. I'm making 'Blossoms' a poem of the week. I just wonder, though, if flowers, even poetically, dream of moons. Write again soon and do not mind my friendly criticism.' She had been referring to a line in 'The Crocus,' 'and dream no more of the love of a golden moon.'

My reply to Dot began, 'Of course I do not mind your criticism . . .' It is obvious that I did mind it. I was convinced that if I said in a poem that flowers dream of moons, then flowers do dream of moons, and if there was some doubt, then the fault lay with the inability of the poem to convince, not in the idea. But, oh, how sweet were the words 'poetic insight and *imagination*.' This was the first time anyone had told me, directly, that I had *imagination*. The acknowledgment was an occasion for me, and, as often happens, this one affirmation led to others, and soon I was being told at school that I had *imagination*. My dream of being a poet, a real poet, was nearer to being realized. There was still the question of a disability – Coleridge and Francis Thompson and Edgar Allan Poe had their addiction to opium, Pope his lameness, Cowper his depression, John Clare his insanity, the Brontës their tuberculosis as well as the disablement of their life about them . . . Well, my sister had died, and the cats had died, and my brother had epilepsy, but for all that and for all my newly acquired or acknowledged imagination, I and my life, I felt, were excessively ordinary. I worried about my clothes or lack of them and my 'fig-ewer,' whether or not I had 'curves' and 'oomph' and 'hickies,' and having read *Ariel*, the life of Shelley, I felt keenly Shelley's probable disapproval of me, for he had complained of Harriet that she was interested only in looking at *hats*. I resolved I would *never* be like Shelley's wife. (From time to time it did seem that my ambition to be a poet became confused with a fantasy of *marrying* one!)

I wrote in my diary, 'Dear Mr Ardenue, *they* think I'm going to be a schoolteacher, but I'm going to be a *poet*.'

30

A Country Full of Rivers

The year of the Upper Sixth was a cruel year, the cruellest I had known. My school tunic was now so tightly fitting that it pressed on all parts of my body; it was torn and patched and patched again, but obviously it was no use having a new one, for I was leaving school at the end of the year. Also, I knew that my homemade sanitary towels showed their bulk, and the blood leaked through, and when I stood up in class, I'd glance furtively at the desk seat to see whether it was bloody, and when I stood in morning assembly, I placed my hymn book in one hand and shielded either my back or front, whichever was bulkier, with my other hand. Because I was now a house captain, I stood in front of Gibson House, unable to hide but thankful that my years of standing almost always alone in assembly would soon be over. I could never understand why no one 'formed twos' with me in assembly or physical education, when the command was given, 'Form Twos.' My shame was extreme; I concluded that I stank.

There in the front of the hall, trying to hide that bulk, trying to remain calm and unconcerned when we sang, 'the blood of Jesus whispers Peace within,' I felt a permanent blush on my freckled, fair-skinned face. I felt impossibly old to be at school. My impatience to finish school and my feeling of horror at the thought of how unfitted I felt myself to be to 'take my place in the world' and my passionate desire to be a poet produced a number of tearful outbursts at home and school. A teacher's suggestion, based on a lone history essay, where I wrote feelingly of Mazzini (our history book said he was idealistic, imaginative – enough to win my heart), that I sit a scholarship in English and history and her disappointment when the next essay, on no such exciting subject as Mazzini, failed to meet her expectations, led to my 'dropping' history, geography, and science, and facing a bursary examination with English, French, and mathematics.

Our class had four girls, the old 'scholar' group, with the members of the powerful group all left to be kindergarten teachers, nurses, Karitane, or general, or to prepare to marry. The girls of the scholar group talked more certainly now of their future university careers and where they would stay in Dunedin. 'St Mags, of course,' they said, alarming me once again with such a familiar abbreviation of the awesome St Margaret's. I was preparing to apply for training college but sitting a bursary as practice for taking university subjects 'part-time.' We were like young birds on the edge of a cliff; wings were fluttering; the air was filled with rustlings and testings and chatterings. The girls going on to university appeared to be calm, smooth, assured, with no doubt of their ability to fly and to soar. Our teachers, meanwhile, trying to capture their own vanished years, talked nostalgically of what to expect and how university had been in 'their day.' We pored over the university calendar, and my dreams had no bound when I turned to the list of graduates and the prizes awarded. I noted particularly the prizes for the composition of poetry and prose and dreamed of winning them.

My last year at school was made more insecure by the arrangements of the class into 'groups.' I was unable to determine how I would manage my area in space, now that I was freed after spending most of my life sitting by command at a desk in an atmosphere that was usually formal, for I had been taught in the 'old' way, where the pupils sat fast while the teacher stood in front of the class teaching, which meant talking and writing on the blackboard and asking questions responded to by the pupils' waving hands in the air, whereupon the teacher chose one pupil to answer, pronounced it right or wrong, then resumed the talking and writing on the blackboard. I was disconcerted to find we were now to move freely around the classroom, sitting in circles, in discussion groups, each member contributing ideas. I retreated. I was afraid to voice my ideas. I had grown used to the whole class being astonished or entertained by my remarks, which I could not bring myself to make face to face.

I was able to conduct the house choir in the Music Festival, 'Go, lovely Rose, tell her that wastes her time and me,' and 'It was a lover and his lass,' and to lead the sixth-form jazz band in:

> Who's the prettiest child
> drives the little boys wild

as a rule they will all declare.
It's the girl, it's the girl
with the pigtails in her hair.

only because there was no disconcerting close contact with the choir, the band, or the audience. I was 'shy,' you see. Was not the Scholar Gypsy also shy?

Seen by rare glimpses, pensive and tongue-tied,
In hat of antique shape, and cloak of grey,
The same the gipsies wore . . .

Toward the end of the year Miss Crowe, our form teacher, gave a sixth-form party for those who were leaving. I wore my tunic. I had my first drink of coffee. I sat aloof in my 'poetic' way (I was now known as the class poet, and I usually had high marks for my essays), obviously dreaming of 'other things,' and during the party Miss Crowe, 'mixing' with the girls, asked me, 'Which musical instrument do you prefer?'

In spite of our one music lesson a week at school and my term of learning the piano, I felt ignorant of 'real' music. The classes were singing classes where we sang arpeggio jingles,

This is the color I like
What do you think of today,
Da Ma Nay Porto la Bay . . .

as well as the loved songs from the Dominion Song Book, 'The Trout,' 'To Music,' the Shakespeare songs, 'I know a bank, Where the bee sucks . . .' songs that never failed to transport me to a place which, I discovered, had been described for me by J. C. Squire in his poem 'Rivers' (another from the *Golden Book of Modern English Poetry*):

There is something still in the back of my mind
From very far away;
There is something I saw and see not,
A country full of rivers
That stirs in my heart and speaks to me . . .

Thus, when Miss Crowe asked which was my favorite musical instrument, I was reluctant to show that I knew so little of music (this dreamy, poetic, imaginative Jean Frame!). 'I prefer the violin,'

I said, thinking suddenly of the blind violinist of long ago. 'Yes,' Miss Crowe said. 'It *is* more emotional, isn't it?' Her reply embarrassed me. Who was talking of emotion? I sat in my corner, drinking my coffee, my face burning with all the feelings and fears in the world.

I sat the Scholarship Examination. In the English paper I wrote my 'appreciation' of the poem, 'Lark, skylark':

> spilling your rubbed and round pebbles of sound in air's still lake
> whose widening circles fill the noon
> while none
> is known so small beside the sun . . .

I answered 'comprehension' questions on Stephen Spender's poem 'Pylons' without knowing the word. I remember these questions only as a result of the intensity of the moment: my fingers were spattered with ink, the clock in front of the hall tick-tocked; my heart rolled against my ribs; my head felt hilltop clear: I enjoyed exams.

The next event was the interview conducted by Mr Partridge, the principal of Dunedin Training College, where I tried to appear bright and teacherly, making sure that he knew I was a house captain, captain of the B basketball team, conductor of the house choir, leader of the sixth-form jazz band, a good student . . . I think he was impressed, probably seeing the bouncy, sporting, uncomplicated schoolgirl which I was not (I the shy, poetic, timid, obedient).

'Has anyone in your family ever been to training college?' he asked. I could have told him about the ever-present Cousin Peg. I could have told him that, apart from Uncle Alec's family of older cousins and Australian cousins, I was the first to go to high school, that my Grandma Frame signed her marriage certificate with a cross . . . then I remembered the aunt's illustrious nieces who had shone in the Deanna Durbin contest, and didn't Iona learn elocution also?

'My aunt's niece, Iona Livingstone, has been to training college,' I said.

'One of our best students,' Mr Partridge replied, looking impressed. 'A born teacher.'

I glowed in Iona's light, and a few weeks later word came that I had been accepted for teachers' training college.

Speech Day arrived. I gloried again in winning, having chosen Aurore Dupin, George Sand, as my subject, making use of her novel *Consuelo*, which Bruddie found in the rubbish dump – yet another *canceled* book from the Oamaru Athenaeum and Mechanics Institute. *Consuelo* with its red cover, small print, and thousand pages enthralled us. We fell in love with Count Albert. My newfound imagination and my ignorance of the actual life of George Sand and the influence of the character of Albert combined to produce in my speech an invented passionate George Sand forever in love with dark, handsome composers and poets, inevitably male. In my ignorance I was not even suspicious of a certain coyness that overcame the teacher when she mentioned George Sand. I – we – assumed the teacher's attitude related to her coming marriage; indeed her marriage was also on our minds at school. I composed a John Brown Parody, which we sang:

> The teachers of Waitaki are teaching us at school.
> Their hearts are full of algebra, their minds are keeping cool.
> Some of them discover now that marriage is the rule
> so they go marrying off
> from English French and mathematics
> to
> Pots brooms electroluxes . . .

The end of the year was celebrated with the usual last assembly and the speech by the invited guest, usually an Old Girl who reminded us that our school days were the happiest of our lives. What else could we expect from the chosen Old Girl of a school modeled on a boys' public school, where we even sang, with identification and fervor: 'On the ball on the ball on the ball/through scrummage three quarters and all . . .,' and 'Forty years on and afar and asunder/parted are they . . .,' concluding with, 'And the fields ring again and again/to the shout of the twenty-two men . . .'

We sang our school song: 'Green the fields that lie around/Waitaki's stately walls . . .,' then 'God be in my Head,' and the Hymn for the End of Term, 'Lord Dismiss us with thy blessing.' And finally, because the world was still at war and we, too, had night blackouts and air raid practice; and echelons and convoys still sailed away; and neighbors' sons were missing in the desert, and others were wounded or killed; and day by day still the casualty lists appeared in the newspapers – we sang, 'Peace perfect peace in this dark world of sin/the blood of Jesus whispers Peace within . . .'

There were many other end-of-term functions that I had no part in – dances, socials, afternoon teas, bike rides. I knew no boys except those next door (too old, and one dead in the war), over the road (too young or too old); my social recreation was the 'pictures' now and again and walks on the hill and along the gully. Although we girls often felt our life had a tragedy and difference compared with the apparent life of others of our age, toward the end of my years at school I emerged from a shocked concentration on the turmoil of being in Oamaru, the state which received so much blame for so much that had happened to us, to a realization that many other girls had not even reached high school because their parents had not been able to afford it or made the sacrifices to afford it as our parents undoubtedly did. I thought of the family of seven children up Eden Street who went barefoot, not always by choice, and of how I'd seen them running to school on a frosty morning, their feet mottled blue with cold; and of the family in Chelmer Street who lived only on soup made from pork bones from the bacon factory. And nearer home, as I seemed to awaken from a long, troubled family sleep, I was suddenly aware of other girls with 'funny' uniforms that were flared without the regulation pleats. I was astonished to discover that apparently K., who was in the sixth-form first year and had been accepted for training college, showed no embarrassment over her peculiar dress and that of her sister in a lower form. We became friends. They were a clever family with versatile talents of writing and drawing; they issued a family magazine to which they asked us to contribute. We obliged once or twice only, in awe of their initiative and talent and their apparent lack of concern over their 'funny' tunics. Once I visited their home and was impressed by the closeness, the almost island state of their family. They were 'poor,' their father, a carpenter and lecturer in carpentry at Tech. and appearing to be very old with a shock of white hair and a habitually teasing way with children: peeping through the hand hole of our red-painted gate, seeing him pass, wheeling his bike (there was a point in Eden Street when everyone had to dismount and wheel their bikes up the steep slope), we as children used to be afraid of his peculiar gruff joking. His voice was pleasant, however. The mother was a neat woman with contained brown plaits wound close to her head. I cherished the memory of the glimpse of their big dining-room table with everyone sitting around it, all drawing, working things out, reading, writing, in a quiet harmony of brown and gold, with no sudden disastrous crevices of being, no epileptic fits, no alarm, confusion, crying, fear. Or so it seemed to us. They had a little brother, Nat, who built and tinkered with wirelesses and could never catch up and didn't see why he should.

Our brother was now separated from us in his confusion. He was alone with Mother faithfully attending to his needs and trying to solve his problems even if it meant only removing the bones from the cooked fish to prevent him from choking. We girls grew close to one another. Long ago Myrtle and Bruddie and I had 'banded' together against Miss Low when June was being born, telling our Miss Low stories; later we all 'banded' against the threat of the health inspector who dared to criticize our home, our parents, and our beloved cats and dogs. There had been various 'bandings' since, and although Myrtle's death had been met chiefly in solitude, June and I had helped each other in our reading of 'Once Paumanok when the lilac scent was in the air and the fifth-month grass was growing.'

Now we were aware that I was about to face 'the world,' with the others facing it also in a year or two. Our strategy took two courses: first, we wrote to Mr Nordmeyer, the Member of Parliament (who had also been a church minister and lived near us), asking to borrow twenty-five pounds to buy clothes and other supplies for our 'future.' We had no reply to our begging letter. The next course was an acceleration of our writing of prose and poetry, which served the purpose of the old Miss Low stories, uniting us against the fear and anticipation of the 'future' which, like Miss Low and the health inspector and the visiting Death, was now in control of us.

31

Leaving the Is-Land, Greeting the Is-Land

It is significant that the last chapter of this volume should deal with
clothes, for it was around clothes that my life was suddenly
centered, even as it had been years ago when I wore my velvet
beastie gown, and as it had been during my school years when I
lived trapped within a gray serge tunic. Appearance had always
been important, and the appearance of others, their particular
clothes, had brought a sense of comfort or of loss. My father's
change of suit color as his change of his brand of tobacco (for he
wore his tobacco like his clothes) could bring panic to his children.
During the depression days my father's suit was gray, and I do
remember a search lasting hours up and down Thames Street to
find a shop that sold a reel of gray cotton to match the thread of
Dad's suit. After the depression, when he changed to navy blue,
our shock and feeling of strangeness were similar to our feeling
when Mother cut her hair or put in her false teeth. In a life where
people had few clothes and a man one suit and one overcoat, the
clothes were part of the skin, like an animal's fur.

When I stopped wearing my school tunic after six years of
almost daily wear, I felt naked, like a skinned rabbit; and the letter
written by the warden of the teachers' college, listing the essential
clothing of a training college student, was the cause of our panic
and approach to Mr Nordmeyer.

I had never dreamed that people in 'real life' wore so many
clothes. As I studied the list, I was overcome by a hopeless feeling
of unreality. Where, except in films, did people own so many
dresses, costumes, shoes, coats? And a dressing gown! At home
there was an old relic, a flannelette checked garment known as
'Grandad's dressing gown,' so foreign to our life that we looked on
it as a piece of history; it was almost as foreign as sleeping between
sheets instead of our usual gray blankets.

From the blossoming wealth of detail on the alarming list I

171

pruned most of the unattainable 'fruits,' leaving the agreed essential costume that became 'jersey and skirt.' I still had my navy blue school coat, and a blouse. These would have to 'do' until I saved enough from my (monthly) paycheck of nine pounds three and nine, and as I was to stay in Dunedin with Aunty Isy and Uncle George of 4 Garden Terrace Carroll Street, giving them only ten shillings a week for my board and keep, I did hope to save money.

And so the future, which had been talked of and dreamed of for so long, toward which our teachers had directed their urging, threats, even their own long-lost ambitions, had begun as the present once again, the Is-Land from which there is no escape, and I was equipped to face it as a shy young woman most at home and experienced with 'creatures' such as cows, sheep, dogs, cats, insects, anything living that was not human; with the natural world of sea, earth, sky, and the plants, trees, and flowers; and with written and printed language with its themes and thoughts and its alphabet with the bowers of A's and O's and U's and D's large enough to hide in.

That summer I burned all my diaries of the Land of Ardenue and my notebooks of poems, although many of them had been published in the children's pages. Only in the *Truth* had I printed my real name, Janet Frame, by which I was now known, the old Nini and Fuzzy and Jean being discarded. Most of the girls in my class at school had also effected their personal transformation as a preparation for their 'future'; some had discovered their 'real' name or changed letters in their old name; others had changed their handwriting deliberately to a new style, often with a new color of ink (royal blue to black or green), with a new signature (practiced carefully over the pages of exercise books). Others chose a new hair style or a new word to use more often than formerly. And yet others revealed that they were one of twins or had been adopted after all.

In our family we rediscovered that Isabel had been born with a caul, which gave her the magic power of never being able to drown.

I, too, practiced my signature. It was a habit my father had, too, for signing his time sheets in an impressive way. He was very proud of his handwriting. He would sit at the kitchen table, writing on the backs of old time sheets, G. S. Frame, George Samuel Frame, followed by two lines that seemed to haunt him, for he wrote them everywhere, on old time sheets, the backs of envelopes, old bills:

> Just a song at twilight
> when the lights are low.

Janet Paterson Frame, I wrote, looping carefully.

In early February, as a member of a Railway Family with a privilege or priv. ticket, I traveled south on the Sunday slow train to Dunedin and my Future.